MONEY MATTERS

utting the eco into economics

global crisis and local solutions

I2270809

Design and Typesetting: Bookcraft Ltd
Editorial: Katherine Pate
Project Manager: Lyn Hemming
Production: Julia Richardson
Copyright © April 2009 Alastair Sawday Publishing Co. Ltd
Fragile Earth – an imprint of Alastair Sawday Publishing Co. Ltd

First edition published in 2009
Alastair Sawday Publishing Co. Ltd
The Old Farmyard, Yanley Lane,
Long Ashton, Bristol BS41 9LR
Tel: +44 (0)1275 395430
Fax: +44 (0)1275 393388
Email: info@sawdays.co.uk or info@fragile-earth.com
Web: www.sawdays.co.uk or www.fragile-earth.com

The publishers have made every effort to ensure the accuracy of the information
in this book at the time of going to press. However, they cannot accept any
responsibility for any loss, injury or inconvenience resulting from the use of
information contained therein. The publishers have made every effort to contact
copyright holders of quoted material. Omissions brought to their attention will be
corrected in the next edition.

ISBN-13: 978-1-906136-20-8
Printed by T J International, Cornwall England on FSC paper.

Contents

Preface

The upside of the downturn: how sustainable banking can deliver a better future

Charles Middleton, Managing Director of Triodos Bank

Triodos Bank is delighted to support this book, in which David Boyle explains clearly, concisely and entertainingly just what he believes has gone wrong with our banking system and financial institutions. Drawing examples from around the world, he describes the innovative ways in which local groups are creating their own sustainable banking solutions – and how these may be the first green shoots of a new world economy.

Triodos Bank only finances organisations that benefit people or the environment – from inspiring renewable energy projects to organic farms. And they do it with money deposits by thousands of savers across the UK. If you'd like to be one of them, visit www.triodos.co.uk or call free on 0500 008 720.

Sustainable banking has been developing for decades, but it has accelerated rapidly as the financial crisis has taken hold. Why? What makes these apparently unconventional financial institutions more crisis-resistant than their mainstream contemporaries? And can they offer a viable alternative, plotting a path for the future that other banks can follow?

Sustainable banking is becoming a significant force in the world's financial markets. The ten best known sustainable banks in the developed world have assets of around \$30 billion, not including the much wider-reaching, more mainstream institutions like the co-operative banks. These commercially solid, growing banks focus on financing environmental projects, social entrepreneurship and community businesses.

Triodos Bank began working in the UK in 1995, following its founding in The Netherlands 15 years before. Today it has offices in five European countries. Over two decades the bank has built assets under management of almost \$5 billion, and grown by 25 per cent per year, delivering a consistent profit. It has almost 10,000 sustainable businesses and projects in its loan book and close to 200,000 customers. That Triodos has been able to side-step the worst impact of the crisis, and prosper despite it, is not a matter of luck. As the core of our banking, we finance sustainable businesses who are delivering clear social, environmental and cultural benefits.

As such, Triodos is directly connected to the United Kingdom's real economy, only financing businesses and projects that provide services and products that people need. In essence, it offers basic banking. A decent profit, a strong capital base and a stable funding base from savers' deposits are integral parts of our business approach. And we think this straightforward model is the way banking should be. Investing depositors' money in packaged and repackaged sub-prime mortgages is precisely the opposite. The issue is not so much the sub-prime mortgage itself. It's the demise of the relationship between bank and homeowner, inescapable in arrangements involving the bundling of loans, that has led to such catastrophic consequences for the markets and millions of people connected to them. Banks bound these mortgages together and sold them to 'the market' but the buyer had no idea what to do if the borrowers failed to pay interest or missed their repayments. The relationship between borrower and lender was lost, and we're now living through the consequences.

How did we get into this mess?
For many years basic banking – raising deposits and granting loans – has meant high operational costs for banks, and limited profits. Shareholders came to expect ever-increasing returns, and substantial management bonuses created incentives for the banks that delivered them. Together they led to a voracious appetite for ever more profitable products and services. This shifted the average bank's emphasis away from basic banking and the real economy, into potentially lucrative but more complex and less transparent products. This led to unprecedented profits – and also to the enormous losses banks face today. Banks like Triodos, which were not prepared to invest in riskier leveraged financial products, have fared much better. Indeed, at the height of the crisis, Triodos Bank grew its deposit base by 15 per cent in just two months. Many of these new customers are increasingly savvy about what a bank should, and shouldn't, do. People who used to be sceptical about smaller banks now understand that staying close to the real economy is safer than being big and involved in global markets for leveraged financial products.

Another factor helped determine which banks won and lost in the financial crisis: whether or not they are listed on a stock exchange. Triodos Bank deliberately chooses not to be listed, not least because the conventional shareholder relationship is anonymous. Instead, Triodos wants to be close to its shareholders and explain its long-term strategy. While our shares aren't liquid on an exchange, they are issued and can be sold on a match bargain market. And the principle used to calculate their price is based on the value of the underlying businesses we finance, not on the vagaries of market sentiment. It is the quality of the loan portfolio that determines the value of Triodos Bank and not the market. This approach is straightforward, grounded in real companies and the people who run them, and prevents speculation.

In contrast, listed banks have to fight the perception of being weak as stock prices drop. And, because they've dropped so far, depositors have become anxious, transferring their money quickly via the internet. This has left some banks facing systemic problems and needing government intervention to rescue them.

What does the future hold?

The past few calamitous months show that banks are not just ordinary businesses with money as their core product. Money, especially savings, is fundamental to the way we live our lives – just like clean drinking water, electricity, healthcare and education. In this sense the banks provide a public service, looking after our money when we're not using it and allowing us to send it to each other. If we do not want to nationalise these core functions, we need bank regulation that is clear and linked to a reliable savings guarantee programme that protects savers' money should a bank go under.

The only way to make sure this happens is to separate basic banking from the extraneous financial functions now offered by so many modern mainstream banks. To regulate savings, loans and payment facilities and call the institution that provides them a bank is simple, transparent and makes a depositors' guarantee scheme affordable. Other functions, like insurance and investment banking, need to be kept separate. This should be the first challenge for governments and regulators alike.

What should we expect of our banks?

A solid banking sector is needed to finance solutions to the real problems we face, especially climate change and poverty. The banks should respond, not least because they can. Instead of generating artificial profits from complex financial instruments and unacceptable risks, banks are in a unique position to facilitate lasting change.

Despite the financial crisis, we're not short of money; we just have to make better use of it. Banks play a critical role in this process. Sustainable banks, including microfinance banks in emerging economies, have proved that their core business works. They service their customers, helping them to become successful social entrepreneurs and contributing to sustainable development. They are profitable, social innovators in the financial sector.

Three important lessons can be learned from their success:

• Sustainable banks focus on the relationship with their customers. They institutionalise the relationship between the depositor and the borrower, not just with money but by highlighting the interdependence between the two. The result is committed depositors who understand what their bank is using their money for, and borrowers who feel supported by it. Equally important, the increasingly controversial reward systems that offer inflated financial bonuses need to be informed by the 'value' of relationships, not just transactions.

• Sustainable banks know their shareholders and most are not listed. The relationship with their shareholders goes well beyond a financial return. Instead they share a common mission. This makes them extremely robust in the face of external shocks, and shocks don't come much bigger than the current financial crisis. Questions of ownership are critical. Either banks can choose not to be listed, or they can choose to follow clear, strong codes for socially responsible shareholding, so shareholders know exactly what they're letting themselves in for if, and when, they invest.

• Sustainable banks are about core banking. They focus on the sectors they know well, financing businesses in the real economy. And they provide inclusive financial services in emerging markets for poor but commercially astute people. Their success highlights the need for a regulatory framework that makes sure banks only work in savings, loans and transactions creating capital as a buffer for depositors – the core business they came from, and know best. Implemented consistently the banks will start to make the margins they need to deliver healthy, effective and key banking services, securing a better future for us all.

Introduction

"There is no wealth but life. Life, including all its powers of love, of joy, and of admiration. That country is the richest which nourishes the greatest number of noble and happy human beings; that man is richest who, having perfected the functions of his own life to the utmost, has also the widest helpful influence, both personal, and by means of his possessions, over the lives of others."

John Ruskin, *Unto This Last*, 1860

Imagine that you woke up one morning and the stock market had collapsed. Imagine that you turned on the radio and heard that, overnight, all the investment banks on Wall Street had disappeared, terrifying ten-figure sums had been wiped off the value of public companies, the Prime Minister was rehearsing the word 'decisive' on all channels, and you were being urged to believe that – even though all the former building societies had been swept away in a storm – the other places you keep your money were perfectly safe.

Nor is that very difficult to imagine, because that was exactly our experience in the autumn of 2008. But outside the front door, life went on much as before. It was more difficult to borrow money, but unless we needed the financial services sector – were trying to get a mortgage or cash in a pension – it was hard to discern any major difference about the world outside. Of course there were long-term effects, but the first sense after the disaster was how irrelevant it all was, as if the gods were battling above us on Mount Olympus, as the great names – Merrill Lynch, Halifax Bank of Scotland – tumbled into history.

But we are all implicated, with our mortgages and pensions, in a bizarre system that operates ostensibly in our name. It is complicated, more than a little insane, and it functions in a dream world above people's ordinary lives – both useless and irrelevant to them and corrosive of them at the same time.

Those who understand the way the money system works (and that seems not to include many regulators) are left bemused. The rest of us feel angry but ignorant. Like most people, our personal arrangements with money are peculiar: however much income we seem to have, there are precious few of us who feel comfortable about our financial health, or who couldn't use quite a lot more cash.

We are aware of the system's contradictions and paradoxes. On the one hand money is an expression of the underlying wealth of the Earth. It has real and powerful effects – sometimes devastating – on people and planet alike. On the other hand it is completely intangible, flowing through the world's computer screens as electronic blips at the rate of $3,000 billion a day, trading in ethereal products – like oil futures or the future value of the dollar over the yen – that have no real existence at all, in quantities that the Earth could never produce anyway.

We can't see money. It slips through every definition. Yet sometimes it is the most powerful force in the world, and can so take control of people's minds that real aspects of life – like trees, people, rivers or species – get ignored completely and then swept from our collective memory.

From the poorest to the wealthiest, we worry about money – we worry about our bank balances, our shares, our retirement, our bills. We imagine that a little extra could solve all our problems, yet bizarrely it is in the richest country in the world – the USA – where people worry most and are most depressed about money.

It is hardly surprising that many of us bolt the door and – like Sir Alec Douglas-Home when he was Prime Minister (1963–4) – wrap our heads in a hot towel and balance our budgets using matchsticks. Or failing that, keep our fingers crossed and hope for the best.

Not only do we feel powerless about our own money, we feel frustrated that the whole obscure business undermines so many of our hopes and fears about the world. The arguments that go back and forth on the media about airport-building, or nuclear energy or global warming, all seem to end in the same place. Money boasts that it can make things possible, but for those of us who hope for a better, greener life – or who want a planet to pass on to our grandchildren – it just seems to get in the way. We don't understand it, don't know where its weaknesses are, don't want to argue in case that makes us sound naïve.

So this book is intended to redress the balance of power a little. It isn't like the glossy financial guides pressed into our hands by sales representatives from banks or insurance companies. Nor is it anything like an economics textbook, full of graphs that are designed to ward off those who have not been admitted into the narrow world of the economics *cognoscenti*. But it will tell you about where money comes from, what it means, and what it is doing to the planet – and what we might be able to do about it.

This guide will not tell you how to invest your money – though it may give you some ideas – but it will tell you all the things you wanted to know that made your bank manager look a little blank when you asked for advice.

It will also brief you for the emerging debate about money after the financial crash – not just how can we get more of it, but what is it doing to us, aren't there better ways of creating it, couldn't we do without it for a while? And it will tell you the truth that politicians and brokers alike prefer not to think about too much – the way they have lost control of a gigantic financial system that could enrich or impoverish us all in seconds if it chose to do so.

In short, this book could make you look at everything from your bank statements to the coins in your pocket in a whole new way. It could even change your life.

Section I

Metal money

Money can be anything you like. The trouble is we are living in a world that is confusing money with real wealth, muddling money values and what we have in the bank with eternal human ethics. And because of that, we are all going a little bit crazy …

What is money?
And where has it come from?

"Money is human happiness in the abstract; and so, the man who is no longer capable of enjoying such happiness in the concrete sets his whole heart on money."

Arthur Schopenhauer (1788–1860), *Counsels and Maxims*

For something we all use so much of, and think about as much as we do, money is extraordinarily elusive. Nobody quite agrees what it is or even sometimes what it's for. At one end of the spectrum it can be shells from the beach, which are used as money in some parts of Polynesia. It can be 12-foot round blocks of stone, used as money in the Caroline Islands – which are unlikely to be stolen from a handbag, but are otherwise less than useful as small change. In Wall Street, money can be screeds and screeds of digital information, flashing up on screens, unrelated to any product in the real world.

It isn't that one of these is 'real' money and the others aren't. All are profoundly real and relate to money's different functions. According to economists there are three of these: as a store of value (like the stones), as a standard of value that everyone can understand, and as a medium of exchange (like the shells – they need have no value in themselves, but help you exchange an exact price).

Money can be something immediately available, like cigarettes, which helps you account for what you need to buy. It can be something a society agrees is valuable, like coins. It can be something scarce that is really worth what it is used to pay for, like gold. It can be something sophisticated and elastic like shares or copper futures. It can be something that can be accidentally deleted by your bank just because someone sits on the keyboard (this happens surprisingly often).

Sometimes it can be a bit of all of these, like the gold that the 15th century Spanish conquistadors found in Latin America, and hungrily extracted from the natives and shipped back to Europe. It is coins and it is debt. It is credit card plastic and it is infinite numbers of bytes in cyberspace – where banks actually keep our deposits.

Except that money is a good deal more elastic for some of us than for others. While the poorest people in the world make do with the equivalent of a few pence a day, the 'masters of the universe' in Wall Street and the City of London (as Tom Wolfe called them in his 1987 novel *The Bonfire of the Vanities*) have a money system that is almost infinitely stretchable. When the rogue financier Robert Maxwell fell off his yacht in the Bay of Biscay in 1991, he had stretched his money so much that he owed twice as much as Zimbabwe. Of all the great injustices of the money system, this is the heart of it: for rich people money is stretchy, insubstantial and infinite; for poor people it is horribly concrete and will not stretch at all. Some people make and remake the rules; some people die by them.

But where does money come from in the first place? There is a popular misconception that the wealth of the world is underpinned by great bars of gold in the vaults of the Bank of England, the Federal Reserve and Fort Knox. Not any more it isn't.

There is still gold in the vaults, and it is still shifted from cage to cage – each one assigned to a different world government – rather than shipped round the world. But that is a historic anomaly, and a simple way of storing some of the nations' reserves. Actually central banks spent most of the 1990s trying to sell off their gold reserves surreptitiously without lowering the world gold price (they failed).

In fact, the pound hasn't been backed by gold since 1931 at the height of the Great Depression, and the final link between money and gold was broken in 1971 when Richard Nixon ended the pretence that the US dollar had gold backing. Now if you read the 'promise to pay the bearer on demand' message on your £5 note, and you take it to the Bank of England, they will simply give you another £5 note in return.

Of course there are coins, but these are made of cupro-nickel and usually worth much less than the 10p or 50p on the front, though recent rises in the price of copper have made 2p pieces worth rather more melted down than their face value. And the total value of notes and coins, produced by the Royal Mint and issued into circulation by the Bank of England and its equivalents, is only a tiny three per cent of all the money in circulation.

Where does all the rest come from? Well, astonishingly, nobody agrees. But most people seem to accept that it is lent into existence by the commercial banks. When you stash money in the bank, they must keep around eight per cent of that loan on deposit – in case there's a run on the bank – but all the rest is lent out again. It then appears as a credit both in your bank statement and in the statement of whoever has been given a loan: magically, your deposit has doubled. It then gets used as a loan again for somebody else. In other words, most of our mortgages and bank loans are created as if by magic by a keystroke; they create the vast bulk of the money in circulation.

And one day these loans will have to be paid back to the bank, plus interest, and so it goes on. It is a magical money-making system that is surprisingly little commented on, these days limited only by the regulations of the Bank for International Settlements in Basle. That is the strange truth behind modern money. We don't mine it; we don't find it on a beach; it bears no relation to anything real, but still some people have vast amounts of it and some people have none at all. And we hardly ever talk about it.

Proportion of global wealth owned by the richest 10% of the world: 85%

Proportion of global wealth owned by the poorest 50% of the world: 1%

John Kenneth Galbraith
Money: Whence it came, where it went
Penguin, 1975

Origins of money
It's not what we think

"The worst thing is not giving presents. We give what we have. That is the way we live together."

Kalahari bushman, quoted in William Bloom's
Money, Heart and Mind, 1996

There are so many myths about money, and the myths lie behind so much of what we are told about economics, that it would take more than a book like this to outline them all. But the first, and the most insidious myth, is about its origin.

We are constantly told by economists and politicians that money began as a way of facilitating trade. We are told that it developed because barter was inefficient and that, for this reason, the drive towards individual wealth and competition that seems at the heart of economics is also at the heart of all of us. In other words, money is just an expression of our inner drive to compete with each other in business.

This is just not true. Neither greed nor inefficiencies 'drove' the growth of money. Of course, barter had its inefficiencies. You have to want what the other person has, and life rarely works like that. The barter schemes that allow some societies to get by without enough cash – like Russia during the 1990s – are fiendishly complicated and devilishly inconvenient (see page 176). But that was not why money began.

Most anthropologists agree that money started as a form of ritual gift – in the form of something you gave the next door tribe when you met, or gave the father of the woman you were going to marry, or gave to your god at the temple. The word 'pay' comes from the Latin *pacare*, which means to pacify, appease, or make peace with. Money began as a way of making peace.

Take, for example, the meeting between Solomon and the Queen of Sheba around 950 BC, where each gave gifts of spices, gold and precious stones. "Extravagant ostentation, the attempt to outdo each other in the splendour of the exchanges, and above all, the obligations of reciprocity were just as typical in this celebrated encounter, though at a fittingly princely level, as with the more mundane types of barter in other parts of the world," says Glyn Davies, author of *A History of Money* (1994).

The origins of money are still there to see if you are sharp enough. In West Africa, ornamental metallic objects known as 'manillas' were used as money as recently as 1949. Some ceremonies in the Pacific still use special whales' teeth or edible rats as ritual gifts of money. But these local 'currencies' have always been regarded with a peculiar horror by modern economists, and officials have even tried to stamp them out. Between 1884 and 1951 Canadian authorities outlawed Native American 'potlatch' ceremonies – the mixture between social, ceremonial, ritual and barter which were the heart of their societies.

What does this mean? It means that economics was never about savage people competing over scarce resources, using money to do each other down. It was about mutual recognition and facilitating human relationships, just as money began with the intricate networks of mutual obligation that underpinned people's economic security in pre-modern societies – and still do in many parts of the world now.

It is important to remember the true beginnings of money in relationships, now that a secondary function of money is to replace human relationships with monetary ones. When things are sold rather than given, when old people live in nursing homes rather than with their children, relationships get driven out by money.

"People do not work and create the economy because they want to support the economy," says the writer William Bloom. "They create and relate – and this, in turn, creates the economy." So don't be taken in by economics. We created the economy around us, and if we want to change it, we can do just that.

Value of ancient Lydian coins today: up to $2,000

William Bloom
Money, Heart and Mind: Financial Well-Being for People and Planet
Viking, 1996

Gold
The barbarous relic

"The customs of the Lydians differ little from those of the Graecians, except that they prostitute their females."

Greek historian Herodotus (5th century BC),
on the inventors of modern money

Herodotus was talking about the first coins, invented in the 7th century BC by the Lydians who lived in what is now Turkey. Within a century or so, the idea had spread to Greece and North Africa. Around the same time the Chinese were making metal versions of the tools and shells that they had previously used as money, to serve as coinage.

The trouble was, as Herodotus points out, that the shift to metal coins was not a very honourable one. It had more to do with prostitution than the beginnings of a great trading empire: the Lydians were actually the first pimps. But it did mean that people could be extremely precise about price and debt in a way they never could before.

Unfortunately, coins confused people about the nature of wealth. The money they were using began as a token of wealth, but soon it became all-important; people believed that gold or silver was the wealth itself, and soon humanity had become caught up in its now-familiar muddle about money. Whatever they know in their hearts, they often act as if:

• Metal money is wealth, rather than a manifestation of the intrinsic wealth we carry around inside us as human beings.
• The total amount of wealth is somehow limited to how much gold there is in the world – so there isn't nearly enough money to go around.
• Only gold – or things that can get you gold – are important.
• The things that are valuable in terms of money (houses, burger franchises, diamond rings) are really valuable compared to things that money can't give value to, such as orphans, nurses, love.

Those errors have led to the most appalling human mistakes. The conquistadors who followed Christopher Columbus to the New World in 1492 set about cutting the gold jewellery off the locals and hauling it back across the Atlantic in such quantities that it caused disastrous inflation for well over a century.

We make the same mistakes today when economists persuade us that money is the only motivation and that only things which can be reduced to money – trees after they've been cut down, great works of nature as tourist resorts – are worth measuring or protecting. "Industrial humanity is behaving like King Midas," wrote Paul Ekins in *Wealth Beyond Measure* (1992). "He turned his daughter into gold before he realised the limitations of his own conception of wealth."

Gold may be a 'barbarous relic', according to the great economist John Maynard Keynes, but in times of uncertainty we still hanker after it. Most currencies haven't been based on gold since 1931. But, quite reasonably, we want our money to be based on something real – rather than the gigabytes of information about debt that it is these days.

There isn't enough gold in the world to satisfy our needs for a medium of exchange – just enough for the very rich. Since Columbus returned from his first voyage, about 1.5 billion ounces of refined gold have come out of the ground – only enough to fill two small houses.

You can see them in bars underneath the Bank of England or the Federal Reserve of New York, each bar worth the same as a London flat. You can still see gold coins minted for collectors and investors, but not in circulation. Gold remains exclusive and scarce, and money based on gold would be the same – accessible by the rich but elusive for the poor.

GOLD COINS FOR INVESTORS

British Sovereign	**92% fine gold**
Australian Kangaroo	**99.99% fine gold**
American Buffalo	**99.99% fine gold**
Canadian Maple Leaf	**99.999% fine gold**

Glyn Davies
A History of Money from ancient times to the present day
University of Wales, Cardiff, 1994

Inflation
Columbus and original sin

"Wall Street, in theory, is the centre of the financial system which provides for the capital needs of the nation. But Wall Street is in fact a speculation centre organised for the purpose of enabling a self-selected minority of men of boundless greed and ambition to become millionaires and billionaires. Whatever Wall Street does to provide for the capital needs of the nation is incidental to, and misshaped and distorted by, what it in fact is."

Ralph Borsodi, pioneer green campaigner,
Inflation and the Coming Keynesian Catastrophe, 1989

The galleons of gold that Columbus brought home caused ruinous inflation. Suddenly there was too much money flooding into the continent, chasing exactly the same number of goods. This is what causes prices to rise.

A century after Columbus, there was eight times more money in circulation in Europe than before, and the reserves of the Spanish and Ottoman empires had been devastated. Most of the immense wealth brought from the New World had been used to buy luxuries from abroad, or to pay off the debts advanced to pay for wars. Its own success had brought down the Spanish Empire.

When prices are rising, the rhetoric about inflation begins to ratchet up, with those who run the government urging low pay settlements. Often they are receiving inflation-busting pay deals themselves. Like the monetarists implied in the 1980s, you might even imagine that inflation was actually caused by people paying themselves too much, which might justify squeezing the money supply.

But this is only half true. Most of us need money to live. If you squeeze the supply of money, the first people to suffer are the poorest. And without money, we all die – "like a peregrination in the catacombs," said Keynes, "with a guttering candle". Economics is in its earliest stages and has progressed little further than bleeding the patient.

In any case, prices go up for more complicated reasons, because there is an imbalance in the amount of money in circulation and the goods and services available. When there are too few goods or too much money, then the prices rise. When too much money was being lent in mortgages, British house prices rose. That is how it works.

Inflation is also built into the way money is created (lent into existence by banks), because it all has to be paid back plus interest (see page 83). It has to inflate just to satisfy the creditors.

More recently inflation has been driven by the price of oil. Because demand for oil is growing very much faster than supply, the price tends to rise and that feeds through into everything else. According to mid-20th century campaigners, inflation was theft. The government undermined the value of our money by printing too much of it. This was true, and is true today in a different way. Our governments have failed to tackle society's addiction to oil, so the world gets increasingly desperate to find its next fix and the prices rise.

Money in circulation in the UK	
1971	£31 billion
1996	£665 billion
2007	£1,500 billion (up 4,840%)

Ralph Borsodi
Inflation and the Coming Keynesian Catastrophe
EF Schumacher Society, 1989

Usury
The great debate

"Those who swallow usury cannot rise except as one whom Satan has prostrated by his touch."

The Koran

Muslims have a concept they call *zakat*, which means that everyone needs to pay what they can afford to help the community. It is a tradition that supports the Islamic belief that nobody should be allowed to starve. Rich people should not press their debtors too far and, when necessary, they should cancel debts.

Nor does this apply only to Muslims. Strip away some of the old stories about sheep and goats, and all the great world religions have similar economic ideas at their heart: letting people rest every seven days, letting the land lie fallow and forgiving debts every seven years. And they all condemn what they call 'usury'.

Usury has been at the heart of Christian debate for the past 2,000 years, and Islam still argues that the charging of all interest is wrong (see page 83). In the Middle Ages, Christian theologians began to accept the concept of interest, as long as the rate was fair. But pursuing people for generations because of unpaid debts, which were rising all the time because of compound interest, was still considered seriously wrong. So was any unfair use of power by creditors over debtors, or any unfair use of market power. It was all considered usurious.

Islamic banks are now some of the fastest growing sectors of financial services, refusing to charge interest but sharing ownership instead. The idea is to make sure that money is productive and doesn't just breed all by itself. But however you define it, usury remains with us.

On the small scale there are the money-lenders and loan sharks who prey on the poorest in society. While typical mainstream interest on credit cards or personal loans ranges between five and 17 per cent APR (annual percentage rate), loans offered on the doorstep of a council flat – to people too poor to borrow money from banks – can amass an inclusive APR of more than 1,000 per cent.

Recent research showed one loan shark charging 1,834 per cent, and even 5,000 per cent has been known. All over Britain you can see people queuing up outside the Benefits Office, with their loan shark who has taken their benefits book as 'security', so they can hand over their dole money to pay the interest on their loan.

Mainstream banks have begun to get involved in the same racket in recent years, bundling up high-interest mortgages with other debts, and selling them as safe investments to the poorest people. It was these mortgage debt packages beginning to unravel that caused the 2008 credit crunch.

On a larger scale, there is the scandal of debts foisted on impoverished people by their own governments and the Western banks which they can never repay. This has led to some bizarre peculiarities (see page 87), including:

• Each person in the developing countries owes an average of £250 to the West – more than a year's wages for most of them.
• Africa spends four times as much on debt repayment as it does on health.
• The commission on the ruinous £55 billion 'mega-swap' loan to Argentina in 2000 – which brought about its financial crisis, and involved 'usurious' interest rates – was £150 million, paid to bankers in London, New York and Buenos Aires.
• Europe used to sell one fifth of its exports to the developing world, especially to Africa; now these nations are too poor to buy more than one tenth.

Yamikinyu underworld interest rates in Japan, money available on the black market:

San	**30% in ten days**
Togo	**50% in ten days**

Henry Palmer and Pat Conaty
Profiting from Poverty
New Economics Foundation, 2003

Bulls and bears
The great psychological divide

"The decadent international but individualistic capitalism in the hands of which we found ourselves after the war is not a success. It is not intelligent. It is not beautiful. It is not just. It is not virtuous. And it doesn't deliver the goods."

John Maynard Keynes, 'National self-sufficiency', 1933

We celebrate successful investors and business people, putting their photos on the covers of magazines, forgetting that they are often just the beneficiaries of economic history. Those who succeed have often simply launched their business in a period of expansion; those that fail – who we rarely hear about – launched theirs in a period of contraction.

The strange cycles between economic contraction and expansion have long puzzled economists. There are regular booms, followed by regular busts – often caused by remarkably similar examples of greed and banking irregularities. There are also 'long waves' between long periods of boom and long periods of bust, stretching over 70 years, known as Kondratieff Cycles, where the expansion tends to be driven by new technologies. Despite the bad economic news, we are supposed to be in a Kondratieff upswing at the moment, driven by IT.

But at the heart of these waves are two different attitudes to the way money behaves, both of which contain glimmers of truth, and which take a prevailing grip on people's minds according to whether the economy is swinging up or down.

The 'bulls' believe in expansion and risk-taking, in speculating in order to accumulate. They are praised for their buccaneering spirit and criticised for their recklessness. The USA was built on an ongoing attitude that money is infinitely flexible, developed by thousands of tiny banks issuing banknotes to settlers, based on almost nothing.

The 'bears' believe the opposite: in saving and security, in sticking to sound money, longing for it to be based on something solid like metal, and for the 'good old days' of gold. They are praised for their solid good sense and reliability and criticised for their lack of imagination.

Switzerland was built by the extreme conservatism of its banks, stretching back centuries.

But increasingly, the dominant spirit of money depends on who you are. The rich live in a constant bull market where they can borrow almost infinitely, and they do so. The poor live in a constant bear market, where it is considered immoral somehow to protect them from their bad borrowing and debt. The rich are subsidised by governments and the poor are sacrificed.

Average proportion of income for UK small business that goes on paying debts: 28%

James Grant
Money of the Mind
Farrar, Strauss and Giroux, New York, 1994

Metal money for the poor
The World Bank and the IMF

"Future students of history will be shocked and angered by the fact that in 1945 the same monetary system that had driven the world to despair and disaster [in the Great Depression], and had almost destroyed the civilisation it was supposed to stand for, was revived on a much wider scope."
Jacques Rueff, *The Age of Inflation*, 1964

The world's top economists made their way across the submarine-infested Atlantic in 1944 for the Bretton Woods conference in New Hampshire, to plan the future financial shape of the world. It was a hopeful moment. But the British plan, devised by the great economist John Maynard Keynes, was thrown out. He proposed a financial system underpinned by a global currency based on real goods. Instead, the American plan was put in its place. The main legacy of those heady days has been the International Monetary Fund (IMF) and the World Bank – the first as a lender of last resort for the world, and the second about reducing poverty to create new markets for the developed world.

They were to become the global police to enforce the rigours of 'sound money' on the poor of the world. Both have remained shadowy, secretive institutions ever since; even the IMF budget is secret. Both are increasingly anachronisms in the face of the vast money flows that shoot across the globe 24 hours a day.

During the 1998 Asian currency crisis, a desperate finance minister whose currency had come under sudden attack in the world markets called the IMF for advice. But it was after 5pm Washington time and the IMF officials had gone home. The security guard told him he would have to make up his own mind.

The IMF may not have been there when they were needed, but they were always able to help some of the most unpleasant Third World dictators, including Mobutu, Moi, Samuel Doe, the Argentine junta, Marcos and Pinochet – all regarded as useful to the USA in the Cold War. Of the $26 billion of foreign aid flowing to the Philippine government under his regime, Ferdinand Marcos managed to salt away $10 billion into secret foreign accounts. Worse, the whole of the $4.4 billion bail-out to Russia in 1998 disappeared within days, siphoned out of the economy through secret offshore bank accounts in Cyprus.

More recently, damaging conditions known as 'structural adjustment' programmes, have been set as preconditions for loans and help. These include swathing cuts in welfare, education, health and environmental programmes. The IMF has also been accused of caring more about the banks than about the poor countries. Its £41 billion loan to Brazil in 1999 had more to do with saving the necks of the big US lenders, to whom the money went in interest payments, than helping the poor Brazilian people.

Structural adjustment has also meant that poorer countries shift resources from growing food for themselves towards cash crops – or anything that could earn the foreign currency they need to pay the interest on their debts. To pay this interest:

• The IMF advised Malawi to sell off some of their grain stocks (they actually sold them all) immediately before the 2002 famine.

• Costa Rica sold its entire genetic heritage to an American pharmaceutical company for $1 million, in 1991.

• The IMF pressed Guyana to encourage so much mining and oil extraction that, by 1998, they had sold permits covering ten per cent of the country; the mining destroyed rivers and forests.

• IMF programmes in Tanzania led to the loss of 40 per cent of its forests between 1980 and 1993.

• In 2003, Brazil's environmental programmes were cut by two thirds to meet the fiscal targets set by the IMF.

• IMF advice to Argentina during the 1990s resulted in the complete collapse of the economy in 2002 (from 1994, Argentina's government deficits were caused almost entirely by the rising interest charges on foreign loans).

As for the World Bank, its fatal fascination with big corporations and wasteful projects, big development plans and big bureaucracies has been at the expense of the people who live in the places they claim to help. It even boasted to the US Congress that for every dollar the USA gives the World Bank, $3 comes straight back to American corporations to build roads or dams or other big structures.

Since 1948, large dam projects financed by the World Bank have forced about ten million people from their homes and lands. The Bank's 1994 'Resettlement and Development' review admitted that the vast majority of those evicted never got back their previous incomes, and never got any benefits from the dams.

Share of votes at the IMF
USA   18%
India   1.9%

Proportion of world population
USA   4.3%
India   17%

Graham Hancock
The Lords of Poverty
Macmillan, 1989

Golden dreams
The trouble with big currencies

" 'Really,' said the Scarecrow. 'You ought to be ashamed of yourself for being such a humbug.' "
Frank Baum, The Wonderful Wizard of Oz (1900), a coded diatribe
against the gold standard and too little money

The great psychologist Carl Jung believed that the Governor of the Bank of England, who presided over the Great Depression, was probably insane. Montagu Norman was one of his patients and he was certainly obsessed with gold.

Norman is said to have crossed the Atlantic in disguise in 1929, for a secret meeting with American monetary officials. He wanted to persuade them to introduce a short monetary shock to force the USA back to the gold standard. Instead it produced the Great Depression.

It is a wonderful conspiracy theory, and there is no doubt that trying to go back to fix the pound to the value of gold – a great bear market dream of money being firm and Victorian – was a disaster. British ministers had such an inflated idea of their own value, and that of their nation, that they fixed the pound's value far too high. As a result, British goods became too expensive and factories closed. And every time more factories closed, the government cut back on public spending a little more. Money was squeezed out of the economy, and life was diminished when people with time and skills couldn't connect with the people who wanted their work; everything ground to a halt.

When he put the pound back on the gold standard in 1925, Winston Churchill painted a romantic picture of international currencies which "vary together, like ships in harbour whose gangways are joined and who rise and fall together with the tide". It sounds a little like the euro, and with good reason. The euro is another dream that currencies should all be the same: it is the great imperial dream of gold again – of standardising money. The trouble is, when you standardise money you standardise people – and that is a kind of lie. And when you tell lies in economics, eventually things fall apart.

In the 1990s, bankers dreamed of giant global currencies. Latin American countries enthusiastically linked their currencies to the dollar, but when the Argentine peso collapsed as a result, they thought again. Linking the peso to the US dollar gave them stability, but it was a stability that impoverished them – because the dollar is geared to a very different economy.

And that is the problem at the heart of the euro: single currencies tend to favour the rich and impoverish the poor. They do so because changing the value of a currency, and varying interest rates, is how disadvantaged places can make their goods more affordable. When you prevent them from doing that, you trap whole cities and regions so that they are unable to trade their way out. Even in Britain – where the manufacturing north is so very different from the City of London – a single currency means that the rich get even richer, because everybody isn't the same.

The euro has many advantages. It will be a source of strength in a crisis, and a useful additional currency for travellers. But when it is a single currency, it is just another dream of gold which can never work for everyone.

So what is the solution? To have complementary currencies that can provide feedback for regions, cities and communities – not instead of the pound or euro, but as well as them (see page 167)? Already the euro is accepted by big retailers across the UK and in phone boxes, so the multi-currency world is already beginning to come about.

Unexpected places that accept the euro
Border areas of Northern Ireland
London telephone boxes
Big stores in Copenhagen
Swiss Railways

Jane Jacobs
Cities and the Wealth of Nations: principles of economic life
Penguin, 1986

Money innovators 1
Adam Smith and free trade

"People of the same trade seldom meet together even for merriment and diversion, but the conversation ends in a conspiracy against the public or some contrivance to raise prices."

Adam Smith, *The Wealth of Nations*, 1776

Adam Smith was the son of the controller of customs at Kirkcaldy in Scotland. The exact date of his birth is unknown, but he was one of the great generation of libertarians and practical philosophers that also gave us David Hume and Benjamin Franklin. He is also known as the father of 'free trade', thanks to his book *The Wealth of Nations* and the idea – which actually he only mentioned once – of the 'invisible hand' of the market.

Smith was a moral philosopher, so don't believe it when modern apologists for the mega-rich corporations tell you that somehow business is a uniquely amoral world where all that counts is profit and returns to shareholders. In Adam Smith's philosophy, business was embedded in morality. Nor would they find much support from Adam Smith for the concentration of economic power, for mergers or for acquisitions. For Smith, 'free trade' wasn't about refusing to limit the power of those who were already powerful – quite the reverse. He was very suspicious of the consolidation of business. Modern corporations, two of which control half of all the grain imports into the USA, would have horrified him. That is not free trade at all under his definition.

For Adam Smith's original followers, the campaigners for free trade in the Victorian Liberal Party, this was a natural extension to campaigning against slavery. They supported the right of free and equal businesses to trade with each other without the state interfering; they never meant the right of the rich and powerful to ride roughshod over the powerless.

Now the idea of free trade has drifted so far from Adam Smith that he is quoted enthusiastically by those who actually have a horror of independent business, and by those who are prepared to force developing countries to contract out their services to them. They forget that Adam Smith's freedom to trade also included a freedom not to trade.

**Number of companies that control
80% of the world pesticide market: 6**

**Number of companies that control
85% of the world tea market: 3**

**Number of companies that control
50% of the world banana trade: 2**

**Number of companies that control
91% of the GM seeds market: 1**

David C Korten
When Corporations Rule the World
Kumarian Press, 1995

Money innovators 2
John Stuart Mill and steady state economics

"A stationary condition of capital and population implies no stationary state of human improvement. There would be as much scope as ever for all kinds of mental culture, and moral and social progress; as much room for improving the Art of Living and much more likelihood of its being improved, when minds cease to be engrossed by the art of getting on."

John Stuart Mill, *Principles of Political Economy*, 1848

John Stuart Mill was remarkable partly because he could read ancient Greek at the precociously early age of three, schooled and drilled by his terrifying utilitarian father James, a friend of the philosopher Jeremy Bentham. But the discipline and isolation was too much for him; he broke down and rejected the narrow Puritanism of utilitarianism in his early twenties.

He was a pioneer of personal freedom, which underpinned the political and economic philosophy of the Victorian Liberal Party that he represented for one term as an MP – proving ferocious in debate (it was Mill who dubbed the Conservatives 'the stupid party'). He was an early advocate of votes for women, proportional representation, animal rights and much else besides.

He also contemplated the idea of an economy without economic growth, fearful as he was that endless growth might create a world where "every rood of land is brought under cultivation ... every flowery waste or pasture ploughed up, all quadrupeds or birds which are not domesticated for man's use exterminated as his rivals for food". He warned against using economic growth as an end in itself, and proposed a steady state economy which had human happiness and development at its heart – where the Art of Living became more important than the science of making money for its own sake.

"Whatever crushes individuality is despotism, whether it professes to be enforcing the will of God or the injunctions of men."

John Stuart Mill, *On Liberty*, 1859

Richard Reeves
John Stuart Mill: Victorian firebrand
Atlantic Books, 2007

Money innovators 3
Keynes and expansion

"If I had the power today ... I would surely set out to endow our capital cities with all the appurtenances of art and civilization on the highest standards ... convinced that what I could create I could afford – and believing that money thus spent would not only be better than any dole, but would make unnecessary any dole. For what we have spent on the dole in England since the war we could have made our cities the greatest works of man in the world."

John Maynard Keynes, 'National Self-Sufficiency', 1933

The Wall Street Crash of 1929 heralded a worldwide economic disaster (see page 127). Even the two greatest economists in the world, John Maynard Keynes and Irving Fisher, lost a great deal of money.

The world then collapsed into the misery of the Great Depression – the extraordinary effect of fear on economics – cutting back and cutting back.

Keynes's solution, scribbling away in his study in Cambridge, was to unbalance the government's budget, borrow money and spend it. "It is often said by wiseacres that we cannot spend more than we earn," wrote Keynes in a letter to the *Manchester Guardian* in 1932. "That is, of course, true enough of the individual, but it is exceedingly misleading if it is applied to the community as a whole."

Politicians and economists urged people to make sacrifices and cut back. But Keynes pointed out that encouraging people to save doesn't make anybody rich; if we all saved everything and spent nothing, we would all die. "We are healthy children," he urged, "so we should spend." Money was about life.

"Over against us, standing in the path, there is nothing but a few old gentlemen tightly buttoned-up in their frock coats, who only need to be treated with a little friendly disrespect and bowled over like ninepins," Keynes said. "Quite likely, they will enjoy it themselves, once they have got over the shock."

Keynesian economics meant that governments could rescue their dying economies, and President Roosevelt learned the lesson with the New Deal in the USA. Keynes himself was exhausted by the burden of negotiating Britain's enormous debt and designing the post-war financial world. He died at the early age of 62. The world abandoned Keynesian economics a generation later because:

• **Statistics:** Keynesianism was taken over by econometricians and technocrats. Keynes was always sceptical of using too many statistics in economics, although he also originated the thinking that led to Gross National Product (GNP). Like Adam Smith, he saw economic problems as moral crises.

• **Governments:** Governments lost the ability to predict spending, especially during the self-delusory years of the Vietnam War (1959–75); the result: serious inflation.

• **Keynes himself:** "In the long run we are dead," said Keynes, when asked what happens when you borrow and spend. But those of us who were alive needed more advice.

• **Margaret Thatcher:** She abolished exchange controls in 1979, as a way to force governments around the world to borrow and spend less. Now if a country borrows what they regard as too much, the currency dealers of the world will send the value of its currency suddenly and catastrophically through the floor.

But Keynesianism is not dead; its spirit lives on, if only in the conviction that human beings can have some control over the money system and that economics is about morality too. When governments only worry about inflation – and are blind to the dangers of depression and fear – we may need to recover his lost skills. Now that deflation threatens again, we may have to re-learn Keynes's lessons.

> **"If you put two economists in a room, you get two opinions, unless one of them is Lord Keynes, in which case you get three opinions."**
> **Winston Churchill**

Paul Strathern
A Brief History of Economic Genius
Texere, 2002

Money innovators 4
Milton Friedman and monetarism

*"He slipped all too easily into claiming both that markets always work
and that only markets work."*

Paul Krugman on Milton Friedman,
New York Review of Books, 15 February 2007

The so-called Chicago School of Economists began as radicals in the
1930s and ended as grand old men of the political right. Their thinking
was forged by the Great Depression, by post-war inflation and by an
overwhelming sense of the central importance of how much money is
in circulation, which Keynes never accepted.

Milton Friedman, the greatest of them all, is now a hate figure on
the political left because his ideas formed the basis for 'monetarism'
and the orthodox economics adopted by Margaret Thatcher and Ronald
Reagan; although these actually began when President Jimmy Carter
appointed the monetarist Paul Volker to head the US Federal Reserve
in 1976. Together they squeezed inflation out of the system, causing
one of the fiercest recessions of the 20th century, but successfully
reducing it well below single figures.

The Chicago economists were quoted by the economic 'police' that
followed them, determined that – no matter what excesses of greed and
borrowing were practised by the élite – the poor of the world should
accept lower wages and pay their debts, even when they were debts to
long-dead dictators, mired in greed and corruption.

The polemicist Naomi Klein also pinpoints Milton Friedman's
economics as the heart of what she calls the 'Shock Doctrine'. It was
the economic justification for some brutal overthrows of the popular
will, including the coup led by the Chilean dictator Augusto Pinochet
in the 1970s, famous for arresting and torturing his political opponents.
There is no doubt that monetarism, translated into the 'Washington
Consensus' – a mixture of sound money for the masses, low public
spending and radical deregulation – is responsible for the widening
extremes of wealth and poverty across the world.

What has largely been forgotten is how radical the Chicago School was in the 1930s, influenced by Henry Simons – Milton Friedman's teacher – in its reaction to the enormity of the Great Depression. Simons believed, for example, that free trade depended on massive trust and monopoly-busting legislation to reduce the size of most corporations to human scale, and major taxation to increase equality. Friedman seems to have believed in the 1930s that all money should be issued interest-free by governments (see page 98).

Friedman pinpointed the cause of the Great Depression on the decision by the Federal Reserve to tackle inflation by squeezing the money supply in 1929. Most of his opponents would now agree with him, as they would in his famous clash with the General commanding US forces in Vietnam, urging him to end conscription.

General William Westmoreland: "I don't want to command an army of mercenaries."

Friedman: "General, would you rather command an army of slaves?"

Naomi Klein
The Shock Doctrine: The rise of disaster capitalism
Allen Lane, 2007

Section II

Information money

Money used to be something you could touch and see. But it is increasingly disembodied, abstract and unreal – stretchable for the rich and concrete for the poor – and in danger of driving out the real world altogether.

Paper tigers
The growth of 'funny money' and the start of banking

"The Currency as we manage it is a wonderful machine. It performs an office when we issue it; it pays and clothes Troops, and provides Victuals and Ammunition; and when we are obliged to issue a Quantity excessive, it pays itself off by Depreciation."

Benjamin Franklin, who printed many
of the notes himself, *Letters from France*, 1779

These days, paper money is actually made of polypropylene. It sounds mundane, but there was a time when paper money was the wonder of the world.

Money that wasn't worth anything in itself, but stood in for the real stuff. It was partly convenience (China), partly a brilliant scheme to add to the world's wealth (France), and partly a revolutionary act (USA, where it was a rejection of British coinage).

Money is also a kind of Pandora's Box, which we can never close – and probably wouldn't want to – but which also brought with it inflation, staggering wealth and many of the other nightmares and tragedies of modern money.

It was simple under Kubla Khan, as the Portuguese explorer Marco Polo discovered in the 1270s, because the Chinese Emperor could simply say what the paper was worth and execute anybody who disagreed with him. But too much paper money chasing too few goods means that prices go up. When the Stockholm pioneer Johan Palmstruch printed notes in the 17th century, he was condemned to death for causing inflation.

In 1716, a Scottish adventurer called John Law escaped to Paris, on the run from killing a man in a duel in London. His paper money – based on the value of land in Mississippi – briefly made him the richest man in the world (see page 125). When he turned the whole of France's national debt into paper money, the resulting bubble ended in a terrifying collapse in the money's value, and he fled Paris to save his life. The incident paved the way for the French Revolution, three generations later.

Lenin said that the best way to destroy the capitalist system was to debauch the currency. "Lenin was certainly right," wrote Keynes in 1919 in *The Economic Consequences of the Peace*. "There is no subtler, no surer way of overturning the existing basis of society."

The truth was that the Pandora's Box had already been opened by the first bankers, who were often goldsmiths. They would make loans or advances in the form of money orders or promissory notes, knowing that they had enough gold to underwrite the debt. But it didn't take long for them to realise that they could lend more than the value of the gold they had on deposit, because people very rarely asked for their gold back. In fact, if they were sensible they could lend out up to ten times what they had on deposit – and let it circulate as money. Such guile didn't always work: in the 13th century the English King Edward III borrowed a vast sum to pay for the Hundred Years War, and then simply declared himself bankrupt. His Italian bankers collapsed.

But anyone who has seen a 'run' on the bank, such as featured in the film *It's a Wonderful Life* – when everyone panics and asks for their money back – can see the risks we run when people stop believing the banks are safe. The collapse of Northern Rock in 2007 caused the first run on a bank in the UK for a century. A global panic, where people lose their confidence in banking on a massive scale, would be an unprecedented economic disaster.

FIAT LUX

The Latin words meaning 'Let there be light' from the book of Genesis in the Bible. Modern paper money is known as 'fiat' currency, because – like God creating the world – governments and central banks create money and simply assert that it is worth something. And we believe them.

James Buchan,
Frozen Desire
Picador, 1997

Central banks
The Old Lady of Threadneedle Street

"I believe that banking institutions are more dangerous to our liberties than standing armies … The issuing power should be taken from the banks and restored to the people to whom it properly belongs."
Thomas Jefferson, letter to Treasury Secretary, 1802

There is something about central banks, which are by their very nature centralised, arcane and secretive places, that invites conspiracy theories – especially in the United States. There are still fundamentalists and strange right-wing sects who claim that banks were set up to keep control of the world's money in the hands of a few élite bankers. The reality is much more worrying.

It is true that the US Federal Reserve was set up in 1913 as a private company, and it still is one – though its governors are appointed by the government, which receives all its profits. It is also true that the Bank of England, which was set up on his third attempt by the financial adventurer William Paterson in 1694, was also a private company – it was nationalised in 1946.

It is also true that the cock-ups, arrogance and blunders by the world's central banks probably deepened the Great Depression in the 1930s, but that was incompetence not conspiracy.

Central banks see it as their role to keep a watchful eye over the world financial system. They can and do intervene to prevent those terrifying collapses in confidence. And so they are often accused of being far too forgiving to hapless and greedy bankers, as they were after the massive bail-outs in Britain, France, the USA and other countries in 2008/9. The question is, whether they can do anything to help us if something goes seriously wrong.

Americans are traditionally more suspicious of central banks, and President Andrew Jackson abolished their first central bank in 1833 on the grounds that it served to make the rich richer. Free market think tanks like the Cato Institute still dream of life without central banks, where market forces can shift money easily from place to place.

But without banks, there would then be almost no institutions left to provide financial stability in our daily financial roller-coaster rides, with electronic money pouring across the computer screens of the youthful traders of London, Tokyo and New York.

Originally, the central bankers tried to do this by buying up gold as World War I approached. By the mid-1990s, the United States had managed to buy or borrow half the gold ever mined, and keep it in the vaults of Fort Knox and the Federal Reserve. And there much of it stays, under the streets of New York City, protected by 200 tonnes of wrought-ironwork around the windows and a private army in the cellars.

The trouble is, this just doesn't work any more. At a whiff of financial trouble around the world, somebody's central bank can totter. Japanese banks have been bailed out three times since the 1980s; the US banks needed the biggest bail-out in history up until that time when the 'savings and loans' (building societies) all collapsed in the 1980s ($125 billion). As this book goes to press, we have witnessed a global bail-out on an unprecedented scale, and it is still not clear either where the money came from, or whether it will be enough.

The World Bank cites 69 countries who have had banking crises since the end of the 1970s, and nearly 100 countries have faced runs on their currency. Sometimes, of course, the markets are right. But they tend to over-correct, with devastating consequences.

Former banker Bernard Lietaer has calculated that in the mid-1980s, if five per cent of the big currency traders sold your currency, it meant a $3 billion pressure that most central banks could withstand. Now, with $3,000 billion changing hands every day, five per cent would mean facing an avalanche of $100 billion against your currency – and no central bank can hold out against that. "Today," he says, "all the combined reserves of all the central banks together … would be gobbled up in less than a day of normal trading."

Since the mid-1980s, the amount of money held by governments around the world has increased to $4,800 billion, but that still accounts for just over a day and a half of global trading. What can we do about it?

- Set aside more reserves.
- Tax currency speculation with the Tobin Tax (see page 138).
- Set up a global stability currency (see page 102).

Money flows every day (mostly foreign exchange transactions, one third of them taking place in London):

1975	$15 billion
1983	$60 billion
1998	$1,500 billion
2000	$2,000 billion
2007	$3,000 billion

Bernard Lietaer
The Future of Money
Century, 2001

The stock markets
The world's Big Bangs

"Speculators may do no harm as bubbles on a steady stream of enterprise. But the position is serious when enterprise becomes the bubble on the whirlpool of speculation. When the capital development of a country becomes a by-product of a casino, the job is likely to be ill-done."
John Maynard Keynes, *General Theory of Employment, Interest and Money*, 1936

The great stock markets of London, New York and Tokyo – and their smaller cousins like the Dax and the Nasdaq – are increasingly the primary focus of the world. Policy-makers, bankers and traders stay glued to stock market fluctuations, or the financial TV channels like Bloomberg, as if their lives depended on it – in the hope of glimpsing a trend that will provide them with an opportunity for profit.

The world's growing dependence on this giant betting shop is disturbing and, through our pensions and insurance, we all have a stake in its fluctuations.

The collapse of the markets in 1929 led indirectly to World War II, but we are now so much more dependent on those market twitches – and the Just In Time delivery systems for our food – that a comparable collapse today could have enormous, devastating, and unpredictable consequences.

In the Irish potato famine of the 1840s, many starved because they only had the potato to eat, and only one blight-infested variety at that. In the 21st century, our dependence on the money system means that we have precious little to fall back on, and the stock markets – underpinning our savings and resources – are the beating heart of this all-embracing swirl of money.

The real job of stock markets is to provide a way for people to sell their investments. Despite the astonishing attention that stock markets get these days, there is a great deal of mythology about what they do and how. Here is the truth behind the myths:

• **It's not really about investment:** The main role of the stock markets is no longer to provide investment capital for business. When shares are sold for the first time, they do. But after that, the share value rises and falls are just rises and falls, which produce no extra money for the business whose shares are traded, only for the pension funds and investors who are speculating.

• **It's not very wise:** Investment decisions are not always made by wise experts, though it may look like that. Much of the buying and selling is done automatically by computer when the markets reach a certain level. And as we saw during the dot.com fiasco in 2000–1 (see page 131), many recommendations to buy made by the financial advisers in the big merchant banks were influenced by whether or not their bank was involved in the share issue.

• **It's not objective:** The markets are not the objective guides to the value of companies they claim to be. The Dow Jones Industrial Average on Wall Street reached a peak of over 14,000 points in 2007, and had fallen back well below that in 2008. It only reached 1,000 points in 1972, and was soon ballooning at a rate of 1,000 points a year, increasing by a third in 1997 alone. Was this an objective measure of the value of US companies? I don't think so. Powerful stock market valuations do not mean that companies are genuinely valuable. They may just be trendy, like the dot.coms. They may be up to their eyeballs in debt just to scare off corporate raiders who might use their spare borrowing capacity to buy them up (the basis for leveraged buy-outs, see page 129). They may just be being used as collateral to borrow more money to buy more shares because the market will just carry on rising (it will, won't it?).

• **It doesn't mean anything much:** Nor are the fluctuations a rational basis for looking at the health of the world economy. Nobel Prizes in economics are now given to theorists looking for regular, predictable patterns in the share markets. Anything from the movement of the astrological spheres to the behaviour of detergent molecules has been used to work out how the markets behave. Many securities firms and banks, especially in the USA, use clairvoyants and astrologers.

• **It's not a public service:** Don't think that traders and clients are somehow on the same side either. "When an account called to say hello, I needed to be prepared to blow his head off and make a sale," said Morgan Stanley trader Frank Partnoy in his book *F.I.A.S.C.O*, describing the sale of a useless Mexican peso-linked derivative issued by an offshore company that collapsed in 1994.

People take the market mythology too seriously. The price of land in Tokyo inflated ten times over during the 1980s, which made its owners into the biggest banks in the world. Japanese companies also used it as collateral to buy up companies all over the globe. The result: overwhelming and unsustainable debt that still threatens to drag down the biggest banks in Japan, and 18 years of falling house prices so far.

Nor are the giants of the Fortune 500 or the FTSE 100 quite as impregnable as they look. The top 100 companies in the world control assets of about $3,500 billion, yet since Charles Dow and Edward Jones invented their Dow Jones Index in 1896 only one company has survived (General Electric). All the rest have been dissolved, broken up by the corporate raiders and their once powerful names forgotten.

THE RISING POINTS OF THE DOW JONES:

Year	Points
1896	40
1914	70
1932	40
1972	1,000
1999	10,000
2006	12,000
2007	14,160

John Gray
False Dawn: The delusions of global capitalism
Granta Books, 1998

Disembodied trading
The unreality of the trading floors

"Like trading ether."
Rogue trader Nick Leeson's verdict on a world where the New York Mercantile Exchange could trade 200 million barrels of oil – four times the actual amount that exists in the world.
Quoted in Dorothy Rowe, *The Real Meaning of Money*, 1997

In the days of the gold standard in the 19th century, the balance of world payments was organised every night under the vaults of the world's great banks – with the exhausting work of shifting gold bars from the British cage to the French cage, and so on.

It doesn't happen like that any more. Since Margaret Thatcher ended exchange controls in 1979, allowing people to import and export as much money as they liked, and since the 'Big Bang' of deregulation in the City of London, the financial system has become a wild electronic phenomenon managed by a gigantic network of global computers.

Money is not metallic any more: it is megabytes of information about debt, shooting around the world at the rate of $3,000 billion a day. And that is why the Chancellor Norman Lamont could describe Black Wednesday in 1992 – when the pound was forced out of the European Monetary System – as similar to "being overwhelmed by a whirlwind".

The financial system is defended not by locks and security guards, but by computer codes. Financial decisions often have to be taken in seconds. Computers buy and sell automatically at different market levels. The real world of goods and services is now dwarfed by the speculative world more than 20 times over.

Trade is no longer the purpose of money. Only a generation ago, speculation made up a third of what was spent on goods and services. Now trade is dwarfed by a cascade of speculation – in stocks, bonds, futures and, most of all, foreign currency – which grows by nearly a quarter every year.

The world financial system is in the hands of greedy 24-year-olds in Wall Street and the City of London, who profit hugely from instability.

Most successful traders keep their earnings a close secret, though it was said that the 'junk bond king' Michael Milken (see page 129) could earn $1.5 million a day even in the late 1980s. Hedge-fund manager John Paulson earned $3.6 billion in 2007. The possible earning power of finance gives less and less incentive for anyone to work in the real economy of goods and services – still less as a teacher or a nurse. In other words, unreality pays.

The consequences for the real world are sometimes terrifying. Black Wednesday wiped a quarter off the value of British business in one day, but the next morning everything was just the same – the same buildings, products and staff at their desks. But a catastrophic loss of belief had made them that much less valuable.

When the Asian currency crisis hit Indonesia in 1998, again nothing real had changed. Yet soldiers threw hospital patients out onto the street at bayonet point because the hospital's dollar debt was no longer sustainable.

Image is central to the post-modern world of electronic money, and so is belief. If the world believes something is valuable, then it is; just as the audiences for *Peter Pan* revive Tinkerbell just by believing in her.

That is the modern financial system, and we have to live with it. But we have to remember that the power the world of virtual money has over us is given by us. We chose it and can choose otherwise.

GREAT MOMENTS OF TRADING ETHER:

1995   **Nick Leeson loses $1.4 billion trading derivatives for Barings Bank, which collapses as a result.**

2000   **Energy traders Enron file for bankruptcy and find that their claimed revenues of $111 billion a year were illusory.**

2008   **Jerome Kerviel loses $7 billion trading derivatives for Société Générale – and becomes a national hero.**

Joel Kurtzman
The Death of Money
Simon & Schuster, 1993

Insurance
The perils of keeping us safe

"It is not in giving life but in risking life that man is raised above the animal."

Simone de Beauvoir, *The Second Sex*, 1949

It isn't a pleasant experience when your house burns down or someone steals your car. But the thought that you might not lose financially – albeit after a few months battling with your insurance company – is at least a bit of a comfort.

Insurance began in ancient Babylon but hardly caught on. It took off in 17th-century London, with the idea of insuring ship-owners against loss. By 1688, Edward Lloyd was running a coffee house where London merchants and bankers met informally to do business: the result was the foundation of Lloyd's of London and the beginnings of insurance.

By the 20th century, insurance was a necessity in the developed world. Motor insurance was compulsory, you needed buildings insurance to buy a house, and in some countries if you didn't have health insurance you would be on the streets if you became ill. The problems began when insurance companies made assumptions about people in different 'categories'.

In the USA, anyone from an ethnic minority was assumed to be a bad risk. Anyone with a foreign-sounding name was refused insurance. One 1933 report warned that even accepting a name like 'Ellis' was risky, as some people with that name turned out to be from the Middle East.

Underwriting manuals used to include maps with red lines drawn on them to show African-American neighbourhoods where no policies should be sold. As recently as 1962, a Manhattan insurance company was alleged to have used maps on which large areas of various New York boroughs were shaded in with a red crayon.

Red-lining was outlawed in the USA, and banks and insurance companies on both sides of the Atlantic vigorously deny that it still goes on. Yet a solid ten per cent of the British population still can't get bank accounts, let alone insurance. President Carter's Community

Reinvestment Act of 1977 forces banks to reveal where they lend money, and to pay large sums if they fail to lend it where they accept deposits. The UK government has resisted anything like that. But insurers are still in the front line:

• The rising number of claims from no-win/no-fee lawyers means that villages and small companies are cancelling events because they can't afford the insurance.
• The identification of genes for heart disease, cancer and other chronic diseases has already led to pressure from insurance companies for genetic screening – and the threat of a new underclass of 'uninsurables'.
• Insurance losses due to the effects of global warming and the rise of natural disasters were £30 billion in the 1960s (in today's prices) – and may reach £200 billion a year by 2050. That might make insurance completely impossible.

What can we do about it? A revival of grassroots insurance for some of our needs along the lines of the friendly societies, the mutual support systems developed by the British working classes in the 19th century, would help keep the big companies on their toes. When the Ithaca Health Alliance emerged in 1997 in New York State, a spin-off from Ithaca hours (see page 182) providing very low cost insurance and mutual support, it faced enormous opposition from regulators and entrenched industry interests.

INSANE INSURANCE
When people from Sherston in Wiltshire faced an insurance bill for £2,500 for their traditional bonfire night in 2002, they were forced to replace the bonfire with a smoke machine and crinkly orange paper.

Peter L Bernstein
Against the Gods: The remarkable story of risk
John Wiley & Sons, 1997

Electronic money
Information-driven globalisation

"We have a problem trying to define exactly what money is ... the current definition of money is not sufficient to give us a good means for controlling the money supply."

Alan Greenspan, chairman of the US Federal Reserve,
in testimony to Congress, 17 February 2000

Money officially hit the information age in 1979 when Margaret Thatcher abolished exchange controls, allowing the vast daily trading flows we see today – what the journalist Thomas Friedman calls the 'electronic herd'. These are not of course flows of money based on metal, or even paper versions of it, but flows of bytes of information from one computer to another.

The last decade has seen that revolution spread to our wallets. We can pay for small items on debit card, making the payment automatically in less than a second. We can pay for parking meters over the phone. McDonald's, Microsoft and a range of other corporates have even experimented with their own electronic money and there are now seven trillion unused frequent flyer points and Air Miles in the world.

Electronic money is a certainly greener and healthier option: it costs £250 million a year to mint, transport and guard the cash in the UK. When they shifted over to the euro, it took 80 lorries a day for three months to haul out the old coins – and that was just in Belgium.

But 'real' money has its advantages too: giving money to beggars is more difficult if all you've got is a card. In a world where corporations know precisely where their customers come from, we may get branded money that, because of the rules attached to it, will circulate easily from mobile phone to the internet and smartcard, but will simply avoid poor people altogether.

But it is the global flow of e-money that is really changing the world. The rapid movement of capital electronically from one side of the world, almost instantly, can inflict devastating punishments on countries that step out of line: their currencies can collapse.

The result is a system, subsidised and abetted by governments, which hands power to a handful of transnational corporations, turning the world into a playground for those who can move capital and projects quickly from place to place. It is the dubious idea that business can make everyone better off by roaming from country to country with no restrictions — in search of the lowest wages, the loosest environmental regulations, the most docile and desperate workers. This is a world of nomadic capital that never sets down roots, never builds communities, and leaves little behind but toxic waste and embittered workers.

Globalisation is many things, not all of them disastrous. The ability to see into previously hidden hell-holes all over the world is a force for moral good. Dictators are exposed. But the rule of one culture over another, driven by the ferocious kind of globalisation that insists that the people of the world trade because they have to, not because they want to, is another matter altogether.

Enforcing this vision is the unaccountable World Trade Organization (WTO), deciding on food safety or environmental impact in closed and secret sessions. Many small countries can't afford to keep delegations there and are thus excluded. The results are everywhere to see, as poorer governments struggle to spend on education or health, or to regulate flows of capital in and out – often imposed by the WTO as 'structural adjustment', a part of debt rescheduling – and their populations sink into pathetic dependence. For example:

• Tribal people were forbidden to draw water from the ancient tank at Maharashtra in India because it had been sold exclusively to Coca-Cola. And the World Bank had been pressurising India to privatise even more of their water.
• Pepsi tried to prevent local people storing water on their roofs elsewhere in India. And collecting rainwater was made illegal in parts of Bolivia after the government was forced to sell its water industry to a US subsidiary.
• The WTO ruled that nations may not discriminate between tuna caught without killing dolphins and tuna caught by those who don't care, or to discriminate against beef given growth hormones, even though they have a built-in price advantage over healthy, natural beef.
• Monsanto prosecuted small farmers for hoarding seeds to plant the

following year – the traditional method. And they have been developing seeds that will only grow in conjunction with their own pesticides.

• Nicaraguan workers were indicted on charges carrying ten years in jail because they asked for a $0.08 increase per pair of jeans they make for retailers, selling at $30 each in the USA.

The symptoms of aggressive globalisation are all around us, nowhere more so than in the enforced dependence of the poorest people. "The imperative to stamp out the smallest insect, the smallest plant, the smallest peasant comes from a deep fear, the fear of everything that is alive and free," said Vandana Shiva in her BBC Reith Lecture in 2000.

The WTO has potential to support the poorest against these terrifying capital flows. But not until it is reformed so that poor countries can afford to use its mechanisms properly. And not until it shares responsibility for enforcing environmental agreements.

COUNTRIES VS CORPORATIONS
From the 2007 list of the 150 biggest economic entities on Earth, the figures represent GDP and turnover for companies and nations.

Columbia	$367 billion
Exxon Mobil	$340 billion
Belgium	$330 billion
Walmart	$316 billion
Malaysia	$309 billion
Shell	$307 billion
Sweden	$285 billion
Austria	$279 billion
BP	$267 billion
Vietnam	$258 billion

Anita Roddick
Take it Personally: How Globalization Affects You and How to Fight Back
Thorsons, 2001

Offshore banking
Where did all the money go?

"There is simply no available skilled labour, and the cost structures are prohibitive for most other industries. The banking cuckoo has taken over the nest."

John Christensen, former economic adviser to Jersey
Quoted in David Boyle, *Why London needs its own currency*, 2000

Where all the money has gone is a mystery worthy of Agatha Christie, made possible by the way that money has transformed itself into information. Where, for example, are all the missing chunks of the $4.8 billion IMF loan made to Russia in 1998, most of which disappeared soon after its arrival?

The answer is that most of it left the Russian economy via the secretive and anonymous circuits of the offshore finance centres, to re-enter the capital markets in private hands, invested respectably in London and New York.

Most of these offshore centres are tiny pin-pricks on an atlas, like Jersey, the Bahamas, the British Virgin Islands or Labuan in Malaysia – though Luxembourg, Switzerland and even offshore aspects of London, New York and Dublin should be included as well. These tiny places now host a staggering amount of the world's wealth.

Because of the secrecy that surrounds them – the Jersey authorities prefer the term 'confidentiality' – we can't know how much. A recent estimate is around $11,500 billion, or around one third of all global wealth. Half of all global trade is now routed via offshore accounts to avoid tax. Once again, it is secret – but at one stage the British Conservative Party maintained 40 offshore accounts around the world.

Meanwhile, vast sums of speculative capital flow through the offshore centres, unregulated and beyond the control of nation states. In Jersey and Guernsey, non-resident companies can negotiate tax rates of less than two per cent, which is why multinationals are sometimes able to avoid almost all tax. Apparently about $1,400 billion is held in the Cayman Islands alone.

Then there are the drug lords, black marketeers and *mafiosi* using the offshore centres to launder their ill-gotten gains. Cyprus alone handles about $2.5 billion a year from the Russian black economy. Organised crime is now worth about $1,500 billion a year around the world.

But even for the small islands, it's risky. Jersey's economic adviser John Christensen warned that the island's offshore banking was pricing out all other economic activities. Tourism is suffering, and there is almost no agriculture left. The cost of living and owning property has been hiked by the offshore banks.

This 'cuckoo in the nest effect' affects anyone living next to a big financial centre – like London. In the end, financial services start driving everything else out. The capture of Jersey by the awesome power of world capital is a warning to Britain, where economic policy is tailored to the financial services industry while manufacturing struggles away unsupported. Perhaps the fate of Jersey is a frightening vision of the future for us all.

MONEY KNOWN TO BE IN THE WORLD'S PRIVATE BANKS:

1986   **$4,300 billion**
2000   **$13,000 billion**

Kavaljit Singh
Taming Global Capital Flows: Challenges and Alternatives in the Era of Financial Globalisation
Zed Books, 2000

Owning know-how
The hidden power of money

"The economy of the future is based on relationships rather than possession."
John Perry Barlow, Grateful Dead lyricist,
'The Economy of Ideas', *Wired*, 1994

It can work both ways. Turning money into information can make it more available: it can help us find out what we need to support ourselves and it can change the whole nature of the money system. It isn't solid like metal: when you sell information, you still keep it yourself – it's just worth a bit less than it was before.

But it can also work the other way around. When money becomes information, then ownership rights get extended from things like land and property to ideas, information, music and words. Both processes have accelerated over the past generation and the growth of 'intellectual property' has echoed with the giant sucking sound of multinationals hoovering up income from its use all over the world.

Patents are sometimes important: they allow companies to invest heavily in new medicines, without worrying about people stealing them once they have got them through the regulators. But the greedy exploitation of rights can undermine innovation in other places. The whole basis of the wealth of some medieval cities was copying and improving the goods they imported. If that is outlawed, it funnels the wealth of the world to the already rich.

It is bad enough when patent rules make it impossible, for example, for developing countries to produce their own generic AIDS drugs. But the World Trade Organization's TRIPS agreement takes this process to whole new levels. TRIPS rules can threaten the livelihoods of poor farmers by handing over control of local plant genetic resources to corporations. By patenting certain traits in genes, seeds and plants, companies can acquire monopoly rights to produce and market important seeds and the inputs needed to grow them. This prevents traditional seed collection and the resulting increases in seed prices can destroy the livelihoods of poor farmers.

The trouble is that TRIPS is based on Northern understandings of knowledge and ownership. It does not protect indigenous peoples and farmers, whose intellectual property tends to belong to the whole community and is often part of their culture and spirituality. More than half of the world's most frequently prescribed drugs are derived from plants or synthetic copies of plant chemicals. One estimate says that if indigenous farmers around the world were paid just two per cent royalties on genetic resources they have developed, big pharmaceutical companies would owe more than $5 billion in unpaid royalties for medicinal plants alone. For example:

• **Neem trees:** In 1994 the American company WR Grace won the patent for a fungicide derived from the seeds of the Neem tree, which is traditionally used in Asia, Africa, Central and South America as an insect repellent for crops. The patent was revoked by the European Patent Office in May 2000 on the grounds that it was not a new technology – but, elsewhere, the injustice continues.

• **Basmati rice:** A company called RiceTec from Texas managed to patent basmati rice grown anywhere in the Western hemisphere – and any blending of Pakistani or Indian basmati strains with other kinds of rice that had been created by farmers there. Basmati rice strains had been developed for generations by Punjabi farm families. In fact the strains had been donated originally to the Washington-based International Food Policy Research Institute. A massive campaign by representatives of indigenous farmers persuaded the US patent office to throw out RiceTec's remaining claims.

• **GM cotton:** Most of the controversy in the West about GM seeds has been about their environmental impact. The real debate ought to be about their economic impact, where huge increases in yield were claimed but never materialised, leaving farmers in India indebted (one suicide every eight hours in the Indian state of Vidarbha alone during 2006), and facing prosecution if they saved seeds as they traditionally had. The real scandal of GM food is about the criminalisation of law-abiding farmers and about corporations taking control of life forms.

The other problem with patents as the basis for innovation is that big pharmaceutical companies tend to invest in research for profitable drugs – small improvements for Northern complaints like impotence

rather than major leaps forward for Southern problems like malaria.
AIDS drugs have mainly been targeted at Northern strains of the disease,
rather than the strains that are devastating Africa.

The problem is wider than patents. By investing in foreign
companies, corporations take a lifetime's rights over them. They are
slowly extending permanent ownership over increasingly wide swathes
of the world.

What can be done to hand back ownership to people, now that we
know nationalisation doesn't really work? Here are three ideas:

• **Rights that expire:** According to the Australian financier Shann
Turnbull, giving permanent rights to investors is inefficient – no
company looks beyond 20 years, so investors are being overpaid. The
alternative, he suggests, is for rights to investments to expire after
20 years and revert to a local trust that would pay a dividend to every
citizen every year.

• **Citizen's royalties:** Every citizen of Alaska gets an annual dividend
from the Alaskan Permanent Fund, of about $2,000 a year, paid out from
the oil revenues.

• **Free shares:** The respected British financial journalist Samuel Brittan
has suggested handing out free shares from privatisations to everyone –
since they did theoretically own the big utilities in the first place.

**Average cost of getting a patent and maintaining it for a decade
(European Patent office):   €32,000**

www.grain.org

Measuring money

The trouble with money is that it isn't a very good measuring rod. It gives a high value to useless things (junk food), to dangerous things (stealth bombers) and to fleeting things (fashion trinkets), but places very little value on the really important things like loving, caring human beings. Yet we give it central importance in the management of the world.

The first accountants
Pacioli and book-keeping

"Use figures as little as you can. Remember your client doesn't like or want them, he wants brains. Think and act upon facts, truths and principles and regard figures only as things to express these, and so proceeding you are likely to become a great accountant and a credit to one of the truest and finest professions in the land."

James Anyon, the first accountant in the USA, 1912
Quoted in David Boyle, *The Tyranny of Numbers*, 2001

The first accountants were the philosopher-priests of ancient times, who kept tallies and worked the abacus, mysteriously and with peculiar ritual hand movements, coming up with answers that nobody could challenge.

This basic measuring system was eventually transformed by the Italian banking revolution from the 12th century onwards, and the Italian Renaissance. The emerging breed of merchants in this period needed to keep track of their international deals while they were making their two-year voyages to India or Russia and back in search of spices or skins, and to see at any time whether they were profitable or not. They did so using three new inventions:

● Paper, which allowed people to write down calculations for all to see, rather than the mysterious hocus-pocus of the abacus users.
● Zero, a whole new concept borrowed from the Arabs along with their numerals. Banned by the Church in 1229 because of its satanic sense of nothingness and its fraudulent potential to increase figures tenfold with a slip of the pen (for example, turning 20 into 200), it was then used as an underground symbol of free trade.
● Double-entry book-keeping, first explained by the mathematician and Venetian friar Luca Pacioli, a friend of Leonardo da Vinci and such good friends with the Pope that he had been given permission to ignore his vow of poverty and own property.

Just as Columbus was sighting the New World, Pacioli sat down and began the book that made him famous, *Summa de arithmetica, geometria, proportioni et proportionalita* (1494) – cramming everything in there from astrology and military tactics to music ("nothing else but proportion and proportionality"). Its section on book-keeping stayed in print for over 500 years and was translated into German and Russian well into the 19th century.

Pacioli developed a way of reducing everything to numbers, but he didn't want accountancy to forget morality and spirituality. He suggested starting each page of the ledger with the cross and the name of God. Merchants had used a similar system for about two centuries, at least one of them starting each page with the words "For God and for profit".

Later generations forgot that basic respect for things which can't be reduced to money, yet accountants still managed to hang on to the aura of priesthood. As a result, failures of accountancy from the Royal Mail Scandal of the 1930s (where they used secret accounts to boost profits in bad years) right through to Bank of Credit and Commerce International (which collapsed spectacularly in 1991, taking with it the savings of many local authorities), the Robert Maxwell affair (the theft of pension money by a rogue company owner), and the Enron collapse (see page 62), have all been greeted with calls for more accountancy than before.

The trouble is that all rule-based systems of measurement tend to miss the point. That is one reason why the tick-box style of American accountancy, known as Generally Agreed Accountancy Principles (or GAAP), failed so spectacularly to pick up the fact that – while Enron may have been the most innovative company in the USA – it was also cooking the books.

Value of Enron in February 2001, immediately before it was discovered to be worthless: $60 billion

Alfred Crosby
The Measure of Reality: Quantification and Western society 1250–1600
Cambridge University Press, 1997

The last accountants
The curse of Enron

"The sense of responsibility in the financial community for the community is not small. It is nearly nil."
John Kenneth Galbraith, *The Great Crash 1929*, 1955

We tend to see accountants as quiet, retiring and objective professionals, and of course they often are. But almost unnoticed behind them stand four global organisations with immense power: the mega-accountancy firms, Deloitte Touche Tohmatsu, Ernst & Young, KPMG and PricewaterhouseCoopers, and they are not retiring at all.

Between them they audit all the FTSE 100 companies and employ over half a million people, with revenues of over $93 billion every year. They are not just auditors, but providers of management services, and purveyors of the very latest management fads, from downsizing to re-engineering. They are also the cheerleaders for globalisation.

The Big Four were the Big Eight until 1987 when Peat Marwick merged with KMG. They were the Big Six until 1998 when another two mega-mergers produced Ernst & Young and Deloitte & Touche. They were the Big Five until 2002 when the Enron affair did for Arthur Andersen, and then there were four.

Enron collapsed in 2001, followed shortly afterwards by their auditors Arthur Andersen, which had been paid $25 million the previous year for services over and above their basic accounting, and which ended the relationship to the sound of the shredding of documents.

The Big Four had just lived through an insane period of corporate history – partly their own responsibility – that led to American accountants increasingly employing tick-box methods of checking accounts that allowed so much wrong-doing to slip past public scrutiny.

In the days when more than 90 per cent of the value of a company like Microsoft could be made up of intangibles – brand value, know-how, belief in future profits – then the world needed innovative accountancy. Unfortunately, it got the wrong kind of innovation. In recent years, the Big Four have:

• Facilitated the concentration of corporate power. When a report found that 83 per cent of corporate mergers produced no benefits, and half actually made the companies involved poorer – though not of course the deal-makers in the Big Four – accountants tried to suppress it.

• Built up cosy relationships with their audit clients which arguably get in the way of proper public scrutiny.

• Aided aggressive tax minimisation for the biggest companies in the world, via legal tax havens and other tricks. They have thus been undermining the ability of democratic governments to get things done (see page 140).

• Intervened in the democratic process: The Big Four contributed $13 million to political funds in the crucial US election year of 2000, including $700,000 to George W Bush. In fact, the big accountancy firms increased their support for Democrat candidates in the 2008 elections, though still overwhelmingly backing Republicans.

NUMBER OF ACCOUNTANTS IN THE UK

1904	6,000
1957	38,000
1999	109,000

Andrew Simms
Five Brothers: The Rise and Nemesis of the Big Bean Counters
New Economics Foundation, 2002

The lunacy of GDP
Why money isn't everything

"We destroy the beauty of the countryside because the unappropriated splendours of nature have no economic value. We are capable of shutting off the sun and the stars because they do not pay a dividend."
John Maynard Keynes, 'National Self-Sufficiency', 1933

The 1955 British general election introduced the concept of 'economic growth' to UK politics. It was innovation of the Chancellor of the Exchequer, RA Butler, based on the work of wartime economists Keynes and Simon Kuznets, who developed 'national accounts' as a way to maximise the resources in the wartime economy to beat Hitler.

The idea was simple. If you could grow the value of goods and services going through the economy by three per cent a year – a pernicious total known as Gross National Product (GNP) or Gross Domestic Product (GDP) – then you could double people's standard of living in a quarter of a century.

The trouble was, it wasn't true. GDP wasn't a measure of the standard of living at all: it was a measure of the value of stuff going through the economy – a very different thing. Maybe all the money was being used for cleaning up pollution or oil spillages, or solving murders, or chopping down trees to make into paper cartons for fast food. GDP would then be higher, but life certainly wouldn't be 'richer' – it would just mean that there had been more spillages and more murder.

This terrible mistake was built into government policy all over the world. If GDP went up, governments could take more money in tax. Soon GDP was the only figure that mattered to officials; for economists GDP was just about measuring economic activity, for politicians it was a sort of Holy Grail. Other problems with GDP as an instrument of policy:

• **It doesn't measure everything:** it only measures success when money is changing hands. If money isn't changing hands, it doesn't get measured. Looking after old people at home isn't counted; paying for their nursing homes is.

• **It takes no account of natural wealth:** when a tree is growing it isn't included in GDP; only when it's chopped up for toothpicks does it get into the national accounts.

• **It encourages fatuous ideas about progress:** Anyone who questions GDP – whether it is better to protect wetlands or forests than to replace them with an airport – is told that GDP is 'progress'.

• **It tries to work both ways:** GDP goes up when people over-eat fast food, then goes up again when they have operations to make them look thin again. It goes up with sales of pesticides that cause cancer and again with sales of drugs to cure it. People in Los Angeles spend a total of $800 million a year on the petrol they use up in traffic jams. Is that 'progress'?

• **It doesn't measure unpaid work:** most of which is done by women and in the home. When you marry your housekeeper, said the New Zealand MP Marilyn Waring in her 1989 book *If Women Counted*, GDP goes down.

But GDP is more destructive than that. Because if that is all governments measure, then they become blind to anything else, whether it is the environment or quality of life. Sure enough, if you don't measure the good things in life, then some get concreted over and soon cease to exist.

By the 1960s, even Simon Kuznets began to have second thoughts. "Distinctions must be kept in mind between quantity and quality of growth, between its costs and returns, and between the short and the long run. Goals for 'more' growth should specify more growth of what and for what" he wrote, in an article for *The New Republic* in 1962.

There's nothing wrong with GDP as a measurement. But it gets to be a problem when it is all we measure.

UK people active in the voluntary sector (not in GDP): at least 30 million
UK people in paid work: 29 million

Marilyn Waring
If Women Counted: A new feminist economics
HarperCollins, 1989

Happiness
Why money isn't a very good guide

"Money never made any man rich."
Seneca, *Ad Lucilium epistulae morales (Letters to Lucilius)* c.65 AD

With all the emphasis politicians and economists put on GDP and growth – and the crucial importance of 'not standing in the way of progress' – you might think there was a link with human fulfilment and happiness.

There is little to link rising income in itself with rising happiness, and a lot of evidence that despite accelerating incomes, the degree of happiness has stayed much the same in Western nations for the past half century or so. Once people pass an income of around £15,000 in the UK, then their rising happiness is usually to do with their relationships with other people.

In fact, one economist who has studied happiness, Professor Richard Layard, suggests a wealth tax on very rich people because their wealth causes measurable unhappiness in other people. There is some evidence that 'status' goods, luxury items and designer logos cause unhappiness in people who can't afford them. They certainly cause envy.

But that is all about relative wealth: there is no direct connection between money and happiness in itself – just between wealth differences and unhappiness.

So why don't policy-makers abandon growth altogether and measure their success in the way that the utilitarian philosopher and social reformer Jeremy Bentham urged them to do – by the greatest happiness of the greatest number? The answer is that it is impossible to balance the happiness of the many against the happiness of individuals (you end up, as now, with the happiness of some outweighing the rest). But maybe they should follow people's moods a little more than they follow money, which they do so obsessively. They could, for example:

• **Help people off the 'hedonic treadmill':** That is the name economists give the exhausting way people work harder, juggle more, stress themselves half to death, in pursuit of material goods.

• **Put meaning above productivity:** All the evidence is that we need balance in our lives – family, nature, creativity – and that the shift from total stress to total pointlessness in retirement or unemployment is a major source of ill-health.

• **Concentrate on mental hygiene:** Mental illness causes half of Britain's disability, but gets only 12 per cent of health resources. Depression is curable, but only about a quarter of those suffering from it get treatment. Evidence suggests that a greener environment and more trees have a dramatic positive effect on depression.

• **Concentrate on public good:** Despite rationing and lower incomes during World War II, people in Britain were largely happier – because of their efforts for the public good. Despite this, politicians have done much to undermine the remaining ethos of public service. The truth is, it makes people happier.

**The top three countries in the Happy Planet Index
(a measure of happiness produced by the fewest resources):
Vanuatu
Columbia
Costa Rica**

Nic Marks et al.
The Happy Planet Index
New Economics Foundation, 2006

Efficiency
The cult of incompetence

"For four wicked centuries the world has dreamed this foolish dream of efficiency, and the end is not yet."

George Bernard Shaw, *John Bull's Other Island,* 1904

Why do trains still break down or doctors and nurses make so many mistakes in hospitals? Why is it so difficult to talk to a human being at a 'customer service' centre – especially if your problem doesn't match any of the available categories on their software? The answer is because these streamlined modern institutions are 'economically efficient'.

This does not mean efficient in the 'old' sense, that they have the resources to make sure people's needs are met, or that they have enough staff capacity in case people are ill. Nor is it efficiency in the sustainable sense, achieving things with a minimum of resources. What is heralded as efficient these days is often nothing of the kind, because nowadays 'efficiency' really means 'value for money'.

The train operators employ just enough staff to provide a service as long as nothing goes wrong. The vast hospitals, with hundreds of different disciplines under one roof, ignore the side-effects of that kind of inhuman efficiency: patients who never see the same doctor twice, mistakes because staff don't feel involved, untreatable hospital bugs.

Of course, it is right that public services should cost as little as possible, but we have reached the point where narrow money efficiency, giantism and technocracy are undermining people's ability to do their jobs. Vast hospitals and factory schools are managed from Whitehall by targets and indicators, often run at arm's length according to confidential contracts with private companies. Defining their objectives increasingly narrowly means the targets delivered are increasingly narrow and the added value – the community benefit that public services used to bring – no longer happens.

The cult of efficiency has been spread over the past generation by the big management consultancies and big accountancy firms (see page 62). They peddle this same mantra of bogus efficiency. The doyen of management consultants, McKinsey's, uses the slogan: "Everything can be measured, and what can be measured can be managed".

This is nonsense. The truth is that everything that is most important – love, health, education, care – can't be measured, so only the less important things get managed. Because it is so hard to measure what is really important, governments and institutions pin down something else, and all their resources get focused on achieving something they never quite intended. Notable disasters of the cult of efficiency include:

• **Railtrack:** Management consultants advised the new owners of Britain's rail infrastructure, Railtrack – privatised for £5 billion in 1994 – that they should 'sweat their assets' (be more 'efficient' in how often they checked the track). The result was a series of accidents and Railtrack's spectacular collapse.

• **Call centres:** Most UK call centres have now reduced the average length of call to less than a minute – then they wonder why relationships with customers are so bad.

• **Hospital mistakes:** Diseconomies of scale are particularly apparent when one person in ten who is admitted to a UK hospital now ends up suffering 'measurable harm' – whether it is from mistakes, bugs, faulty equipment or drug side-effects.

Ironically, these 'externalities' (see page 75) make these vast new bureaucracies expensive to run, but the real bill falls on someone else.

Cost of additional hospital stays required because of hospital mistakes: £2 billion a year

David Boyle
The Tyranny of Numbers
HarperCollins/Flamingo, 2001

Measuring what is important 1
Alternative indicators

"If your local police chief announced that 'activity' on the streets had increased by 15%, people would not be interested. Exactly what increased? Tree planting or burglaries? Volunteerism or muggings? Car wrecks or neighborly acts of kindness?"

Atlantic Monthly, October 1995

There must be better ways of measuring progress than just money, and there are. Bhutan uses a measure they call 'gross national contentment'.

A group of researchers from the think tank Redefining Progress put forward an alternative in the American magazine *Atlantic Monthly*. Their article piled on the evidence against GDP. The *Wall Street Journal* had just worked out that OJ Simpson's trial in 1995 had cost the equivalent of the total GDP of Grenada. Was that progress? Then there were the liposuction operations – 110,000 of which take place every year in the USA, each of them pumping $2,000 into the growth figures.

Their solution was called the Index of Sustainable Economic Welfare (ISEW), which they plotted against GDP on a chart. The ISEW showed that while GDP went up inexorably, sustainable welfare changed direction in the 1970s and started going down. The ISEW for the UK showed a similar decline. In other words, if you ignore the bottom line of money, we are actually worse off. We are suffering from the opposite of wealth, what John Ruskin called 'illth'.

The ISEW launched a worldwide movement to measure progress more meaningfully. Cities began to use different yardsticks. Seattle used the number of salmon in local streams, the number of books taken out of local libraries and the ratio between burger and vegetarian restaurants. Such indicators became central to Seattle's planning for the future.

In the UK, there was a similar story. Local authorities tried measuring the number of breeding golden eagles (Strathclyde), the asthma rate (Leeds), the amount sold in small shops (West Devon), the number of swans (Norwich). None of them were enough by themselves, but these alternative indicators have been an important counterweight to the narrowness of money. No one measure can sum up all the facets of 'wealth', but these indicators did at least broaden the debate.

The problem is that governments have transformed these useful indicators into concrete targets by which they can control the way their outlying agencies and grant recipients do their jobs – while still relying on economic growth as their main indicator of success. So are alternative indicators still useful? And what should we do?

• **Refuse to accept centralised targets wherever possible:** They interfere with real progress and fail to understand the critical relationships between people on the ground, which is the basis of beneficial change.

• **Measure what matters to people:** not what central government tells us to measure.

• **Measure hot indicators:** The city in Peru that chose an indicator of air quality based not on something that scientists had to test, but on whether or not they could see the Andes, were proposing something much more meaningful to people.

• **Get broadcasters to include indicators in weather reports:** the green economist Hazel Henderson got New York broadcasters to do this with air quality in the 1960s.

• **Force politicians to hold the government to account:** make them account for what is really important, not measures of bogus efficiency like GDP.

A USEFUL INDICATOR
Population of the USA: 290 million
Number of fast food outlets in the USA: 300,000

Alex MacGillivray, Candy Weston, and Catherine Unsworth
Communities Count! A step-by-step guide to community sustainability indicators
New Economics Foundation, 1998

Measuring what is important 2
Social auditing

"Business must be run at a profit, else it will die. But when anyone tries to run a business solely for profit ... then also the business must die, for it no longer has a reason for existence."

Henry Ford, *Today and Tomorrow*, 1926

The Dutch West India Company's 1621 charter made it responsible for conservation, police and justice. If you had economic power in those days, you were expected to have moral responsibilities. Over the past century or so, business philosophy has forgotten that crucial truth, and we can see the results all around us in the devastated environment, poisoned children and degraded lives.

We need a solution to this moral blindness all the more urgently now that the world's largest corporations account for as much as 28 per cent of global activity, yet only pay 0.25 per cent of the world's population as employees. As their monopoly on economic activity gets sharper, it is harder for anyone to sustain themselves outside their corrosive embrace.

Social auditing has emerged over the past quarter of a century as a different way of measuring companies' success. It demands that they look beyond their shareholders to measure their impact on a range of other 'stakeholders' – anyone from employees and their families to regulators, suppliers, neighbours, customers and the environment.

John Elkington, co-author of the 1988 bestseller *The Green Consumer Guide* (see page 202), had the idea that every company should have what he called a 'triple bottom line' for their economic, environmental and social achievement. It was all a long way from the days when one of the American 'robber baron' capitalists, Cornelius Vanderbilt, used to keep all his company's figures in his head because he didn't trust anybody.

In the atmosphere of corporate suspicion of the 1990s, social auditing became unexpectedly popular. One new social auditing consultancy reported 50 enquiries a day. Soon the social audits or the unaudited social reports, like the Shell Values report, were pouring off the presses, full of glossy pictures and lofty claims: "We had looked in the mirror and we neither recognised nor liked what we saw," said the Shell Values report. "We have set about putting it right."

Do we believe them? Not quite yet. Social auditing still has some way to go before it becomes mainstream; here are some of its faults:

• **Too much greenwash:** Some social reports are glossy PR efforts that hide the basic unsustainability of everything else the company is doing.
• **Too many numbers:** Social auditing has tended to shift responsibility for ethics away from chief executives and over to number-crunchers in the audit department – and, after all, you can't actually measure what's really important.
• **Too vague:** Different social reports use different measures. They need to be simpler and more standard before they attract widespread interest.
• **Too irrelevant:** Corporate social responsibility remains stuck, because the basic controls on a company are still share price and the money markets – and any company that tries to be more ethical than others, like Levi-Strauss or the Body Shop, can be seriously punished by the financiers and the traders.

A new category of business is emerging, whose core purpose is rescuing the world. Authentic companies like Good Energy who provide green energy in the UK, are not having to compromise in the way that the winners of green business awards did a decade ago, showing that they were green despite their core activity. It may be that authentic companies will eventually push out the old ones, but that may be too long to wait.

Amount of global food marketing aimed directly at children in the USA, despite criticisms of its irresponsibility: $18 billion

Jonathon Porritt
Capitalism as if the World Matters
Earthscan, 2005

Other kinds of capital
Why it isn't just about money

"How much would it cost you in real cash terms if none of your employees had ever been toilet-trained?"
Alvin Toffler, questioning senior US corporate executives

Even the money system grinds to a halt if some of its support structures start to look threadbare. Old-fashioned economics used to imagine three kinds of capital – land, labour and 'manufactured capital', by which they meant factories, machines, tools and homes. But green economists like Paul Ekins have replaced that with a model of four pillars that underpin real wealth:

• **Manufactured capital:** the importance of the buildings we live in, and the infrastructure. We can't make the economy work if the trains keep breaking down.

• **Environmental capital:** however much money we might have, we will be grindingly poor if we can't breathe the air and we are the only species on the planet left alive.

• **Intellectual capital:** the vital importance of ideas and know-how. If companies don't treat their staff well, their knowledge may just walk out of the door and work for their competitors.

• **Social capital:** everything we do depends on our having supportive families and neighbourhoods. Doctors can't make people well without the co-operation of their patients and the wider community, the police can't tackle crime and violence, and business profits evaporate if the community malfunctions.

One study of social capital found that the number of times tenants visited their GP depended on whether the council scheme to demolish their homes was on or off. And in a massive study in Chicago in 1997, researchers found that the crime rate in each neighbourhood had nothing to do with income or unemployment: it was about whether people felt safe enough to intervene when they saw children and teenagers hanging around.

There in a nutshell is the problem of modern money: it ignores people and the environment. Their destruction as a by-product of economic activity is blandly called an 'externality'. Yet while small diverse shops nurture social capital, big supermarkets drive it out.

THE VALUE OF SMALL SHOPS

"One ordinary morning last winter, Bernie Jaffe and his wife Ann supervised the small children crossing at the corner [on the way to school]; lent an umbrella to one customer and a dollar to another; took in some packages for people who were away; lectured two youngsters who asked for cigarettes; gave street directions; took custody of a watch to give to the repair man across the street; gave out information on the range of rents in the neighbourhood to an apartment seeker; listened to a tale of domestic difficulty and offered reassurance; told some rowdies they could not come in unless they behaved and then defined (and got) good behaviour; provided an incidental forum for half a dozen conversations among customers who dropped in for oddments; set aside certain newly arrived papers and magazines for regular customers; advised a mother who came for a birthday present not to get the ship-model kit because another child going to the same birthday party was giving that; and got a back copy (this was for me) of the previous day's newspaper out of the deliverer's surplus returns when he came by."

Jane Jacobs, *The Death and Life of Great American Cities*, 1961

Paul Ekins, Mayer Hillman, and Robert Hutchison
Wealth Beyond Measure: An atlas of new economics
Gaia Books, 1992

Green taxes
Taxing the bad things

" 'It was as true as taxes is,' said Mr Barkis, '… as taxes is. And nothing's truer than them.' "

Charles Dickens, *David Copperfield*, 1850

What can we do about this damage to the fabric of the world, these so-called externalities, that seem to be produced by most economic activity? Some you can make illegal, but some you simply can't. Some you can tax, and at the same time shift taxes off good things like jobs or added value. This would mean that polluters had to pay for their damage.

Even the laggardly British government has successfully taxed petrol, use of landfill for waste disposal, and now traffic congestion in London. But to tax effectively you have to know what the damage is worth – not precisely, but, for political reasons you need some facts at your fingertips.

Taxes on cars and petrol in the UK raise around £42 billion, but – contrary to popular opinion – this doesn't cover the real damage that road traffic causes. According to the environmental economist David Pearce, once you have factored in policing, health effects, the cost of injuries and deaths on the roads, the effects of increasing greenhouse gases on the climate, the bill is far nearer £53 billion (that was at 1995 prices). In other words, we are all subsidising the drivers on the roads.

Like all taxes, green taxes are not popular. But everyone understands the sense in them, and – for good political reasons – it is sensible to cut other taxes. But green taxes do have another problem: they are designed both to raise money and to reduce pollution, so you can't entirely predict their effects. The more effective they are in persuading people not to drive or to smoke, the less money they will yield, so they need to be backed by other taxes that are more predictable. Future green taxes could include:

• **Land:** Land taxes – on site value – would reduce wasted land. (They nearly became law in the UK twice, in 1915 and 1931.) Now they could raise about £50 billion a year in the UK alone, though by encouraging development, land taxes might make cities less green.

- **Rubbish:** The British government's landfill tax is underpinned by the European Union, which will fine the UK £500,000 if it misses targets for reducing rubbish dumping.
- **Obsolescence**: Manufacturers of toasters, tumble dryers and even kettles in Europe are now responsible for the recycling of their products. Even so, about 5 million perfectly good computers are currently put into UK landfill every year.
- **Plastic bags:** The Irish tax of 10p per plastic carrier bag has cut their use by over 90 per cent.
- **Energy:** The so-called Unitax – a single tax that replaces all others on energy at the point of sale – has been proposed as the most effective and least avoidable tax. No sign of it yet, though.
- **Out of town parking:** Out of town superstores have the benefit over town centres of letting people park for free. A tax on each parking space would even up the balance.
- **Currency speculation:** The proposal by the Nobel Prize-winning economist James Tobin for a tax of 0.05 per cent on speculative currency flows (see page 138) might be the only way of raising enough for the UN to implement its sustainable development ambitions.

Number of plastic bags used around the world every minute: about 1 million

David Pearce and Edward B Barbier
Blueprint for a Sustainable Economy
Earthscan, 2000

Cost–benefit analysis
Knowing the price of everything

"A man who knows the price of everything and the value of nothing."
Oscar Wilde's definition of a cynic, *Lady Windermere's Fan*, 1892

Measuring the costs or benefits of some of the side-effects of money –
on health or the environment – is vital if you want to persuade people
about damage to the planet. To convince people that taxing aviation fuel
(currently exempt) is a good idea, you need to calculate the real costs of
flying: the pollution, the concrete, the road traffic, the greenhouse effect
and much more.

But there are problems in calculating the price of health or the
environment. Cost–benefit analysis began as a way for French railway
engineers to work out what to charge for railway tickets on new lines
in the 1840s, and was developed by the US Army Corps of Engineers
as a way to take the politics out of dam-building decisions in the 1930s.
It became part of the modern fantasy that decisions can be made
'scientifically' by technocrats, without recourse to discussion.

The biggest cost–benefit analysis ever was carried out in the late
1960s to work out where to build the third London Airport. Critics
said that if you really took such calculations seriously, it would be
cheaper to build it in Hyde Park, but Westminster Abbey would have
to be demolished. (A retired air marshal wrote to the *Daily Telegraph*
to say he had been arguing the Hyde Park case for years.) During this
process, economists valued the medieval church at Cublington in
Buckinghamshire at £51,000 – ten times that at today's prices – if it was
demolished. In the event, the airport was built at Stansted.

Modern cost–benefit analysis uses the amount of money people are
willing to pay to save whales or the Grand Canyon, for example. The
idea is to find some basis for international negotiations, but the danger
is that economists might really believe the price is real – although such
things as species, life, beauty are actually priceless.

Still, economists have worked out that all the elephants are worth
$100 million, or that the Grand Canyon was worth $4.43 per person

per month, or that an American life is worth 15 times more than a Chinese life. The danger is that these prices could seep out of political negotiations and on to company or national balance sheets. Already the world economy values an Albanian orphan at £4,000 and a reasonably sized house in central London at over £1 million. People really believe these things.

Nor can you really measure willingness to pay. About a quarter of people who were asked what they would be willing to pay to preserve bald eagles, woodpeckers, coyotes, salmon or wild turkeys refused to reply on the grounds that you just can't put a price on such things. Of course you can't.

A Frankfurt woman called Frau Kraus discovered in 1989 that she had a veto over a proposed new skyscraper planned next door, and refused to play the game at all. She turned down one million deutschmarks, then she turned down ten million. "Not even if they were to offer me 20 million would I change my mind," she told the papers. "It would block out my sunlight and spoil the place I was born and bred."

SHOCKING COST–BENEFIT
In 1973, Ford worked out that it would cost $137 million to recall the Ford Pinto (liable to burst into flames when it was hit from behind) but only $49 million to settle wrongful death lawsuits. They were punished in the courts in 1981.

John Adams
Cost–Benefit Analysis: Part of the problem, not the solution
Green College, Oxford, 1995

Corporate subsidies
Welfare for the richest

"The annual total of perverse subsidies is larger than all but the five leading national economies, larger than the top 12 corporations' annual sales, and ... twice as large as annual global military spending."

Norman Myers, Royal Society of Arts lecture, 2000

Green taxes are a step in the right direction, but they are a drop in the ocean compared to the taxes we pay to subsidise activities that damage people and planet. While our leaders claim to be working for sustainability, the economic system does the opposite. Who is paying for all this terrifying damage to the planet? We all are.

There are hidden health or environmental costs as a result, and these have to be paid for too. Sometimes, like the health costs due to increased traffic, they are not paid for properly. Sometimes the real cost to future generations is impossible to calculate – like the future effects of encouraging traffic by building roads, or of encouraging air travel by building runways and giving tax breaks for air fuel; or the long-term effects of subsidising nuclear energy; or the long-term effects on children of encouraging a global culture of endless consumerism, fast food and high pressure marketing.

The UK government spends over £6 billion a year on roads, but how much does it cost the NHS to treat the people made ill by traffic pollution? We don't know, but Friends of the Earth estimates that about one in 50 heart attacks in London is a direct result of traffic pollution. How much of the £6 billion which bad diet costs the NHS annually is as a result of tax breaks given to supermarkets? According to the agricultural economist Jules Pretty, externalities in agriculture mean we pay for our food three times over – once in the shops, once as taxpayers for the subsidy and once as taxpayers to clean up some of the mess from the way it is produced. The situation is even worse elsewhere:

• **Food:** About a fifth of the $20 billion annual subsidies that the US government pays to farmers goes to big corporate factory farms.

• **Energy:** The European Commission has agreed to carry on subsidising six coal mines in Germany until 2010. Nuclear energy also relies on massive subsidies, not least for clean-up and decommissioning of nuclear power plants.

• **Fisheries:** Worldwide, ocean fisheries cost more than £66 billion a year, but the fish are sold for about £48 billion. The worldwide shortfall is funded by governments, which thus contribute to making commercial fishing almost extinct.

In 2001, the green economist Norman Myers worked out that corporate subsidies worldwide totalled around £1,200 billion in a global economy worth £18,000 billion, mainly to support agriculture, fossil fuels, nuclear energy, road transport, water and fisheries. There are 40,000 lobbyists in Brussels alone, making sure this corporate featherbedding continues.

Subsidy paid to the investment bank Goldman Sachs to build their new corporate headquarters in New York: $650 million

World Bank support for transport

Roads	**98%**
Rail	**2%**
Cycling	**nothing**

Norman Myers and Jennifer Kent
Perverse Subsidies: How misused tax dollars harm the environment and the economy
Island Press, 2001

Section IV

Debt money

Where did all the money go? There's enough to create tidal waves around the world financial system, but not enough – it seems – for the important things in life, such as small shops and healthy food or local buses and local police. Why is this? It may have something to do with debt ...

The hidden flaw in money
The trouble with interest

"It is amazing that this monster interest has not devoured the whole of humanity. It would have done so long ago had not bankruptcy and revolution acted as counter-poisons."

Napoleon Bonaparte, quoted in Michael Flurscheim,
Clue to the Economic Labyrinth, 1902

There is something rather miraculous about modern money: it grows all by itself.

Certainly, compound interest is miraculous if you're on the right side of it. It makes pensions possible. It means we no longer have workhouses. And it gives you a warm feeling inside as you watch the money in your savings account slowly breed.

But if you are in debt, the idea of compound interest is much less comfortable. From individuals to developing countries, every time you look at the debt bill, it seems even bigger. Compound interest is wonderful for people with money, and a burden for those without. It is the miracle and the fatal flaw at the heart of the money system.

But the traditional critique of charging interest, which goes back to the teachings of Christianity and Islam, is that it is unnatural for money to make money out of money. Eco-systems increase at a natural rate, accelerated by humankind but within limits. But the interest at the heart of money demands returns that the natural world simply can't supply. Charging interest on money – rather than charging a simple fee for arranging a loan, as the Islamic banks do – drives unsustainability. The world can no longer stand still: it has to increase consumption and environmental destruction just to pay the interest.

Most major religions still condemn 'usury', although Christianity and Judaism allow a reasonable percentage. But Islam sticks to the original interpretation– and it has a point. According to the German architect Margrit Kennedy, a penny invested at average rates of interest at the time of Christ would now be worth nearly 9,000 balls of gold, each equal to the weight of the Earth. "The economic necessity and the mathematical impossibility create a contradiction ... which has led to innumerable feuds, wars and revolutions in the past," she says.

That's the danger of charging interest. Since most money in circulation is created via loans from banks (see page 13), then nearly all money – except the notes and coins in our pockets – carries this burden because some day it has to be paid back, plus interest. Nature isn't like that: it doesn't grow nearly so fast. "The assumption is that growth is good and more is better," says the green economist Paul Ekins in *Wealth Beyond Measure*. "It's as if economists have never heard of cancer."

Islamic banking is now one of the fastest growing sectors of financial services. Even HSBC and Citibank have opened Islamic operations in the Persian Gulf, and HSBC offers Islamic mortgages in New York. Islamic banks don't charge interest when they lend money, but take part ownership instead. So money invested in an Islamic bank keeps 'working'. If the bank invests in a weak business then it may lose money even if the loan is repaid.

The success of Islamic banking, and of the Scandinavian interest-free bank JAK, shows that there is a demand for interest-free banking, which may become a larger part of the financial system.

**If Christ had invested a penny at 4% interest,
it would have bought:**
1750   a ball of gold equal to the weight of the Earth.
1990   8,190 balls of gold the same size.

Margrit Kennedy, with Declan Kennedy
Interest and Inflation Free Money
New Society, 1995

Mortgages
The death grip

"Slavery they can have anywhere. It is a weed that grows in every soil."
Edmund Burke, second speech on conciliation with America, 1775

When people complain that dinner party conversation is obsessed
with the value of people's homes, we assume that staying glued to the
window of the estate agents – watching prices rise or fall – somehow
means being obsessed with trivia. And it is, in a sense. But in another
sense, house prices and the mortgages that drive them are more
important than we often realise, because:

• **They are not based on real values:** The extraordinary rise in house
prices in Britain – from an average UK price of £5,000 in 1970 to over
£200,000 today – has led to a massive shift in value from one generation
to the next. Thousands of ordinary people become millionaires simply
from the sale of their parents' homes. But when houses are used as
security for other loans we should beware, because house prices are not
real. My small house is, apparently, worth far more than would actually
be needed to rebuild it.
• **They force up house prices:** House prices are supposed to rise
because of supply and demand, but now that homes are increasingly
used as investments that is only partly true. What really drives up house
prices is the supply and demand of mortgage finance. Tokyo house
prices multiplied ten times over in the 1980s because 'grandparent
mortgages' were invented, whereby the money would be paid off in two
generations' time. Tokyo houses remain the most expensive in the world.
• **We need mortgages more than we know:** As much as two thirds
of the money in circulation in Britain was originally created as mortgage
loans. If we didn't have high house prices – under current arrangements
at least – our money would dry up.
• **We can never pay them off:** It may be possible for us to pay off
our mortgages individually, but as a community we never will – partly
because the nation needs the money in circulation, and partly because

there may not be enough money in circulation to pay it off. In the UK we have total debts (including mortgages) of over £1.4 trillion – and only around £1.3 trillion in circulation.

The word mortgage means 'death grip' or 'death promise' and used to be a last-resort method of raising money, using your property as collateral. Even in the early years of widespread home ownership in the 1930s, with affordable semi-detached houses widely available, most mortgages were for 15 years and took less than one tenth of your salary. They were also usually paid off early.

These days, mortgage payments can take up well over a third of your income, and most of us can only afford houses in the first place if two people are earning to pay it off. About 37 per cent of the UK housing stock is mortgaged, and it is more and more difficult to get on the bottom rung of the housing ladder.

It is a strange paradox that the houses were built and paid for long ago, yet we own fewer and fewer of them as time goes by. Why should a third of all Britain's housing stock be owned by the mortgage lenders? If they stop lending, the housing market dries up, locking people into their existing address. But every time financial institutions lend more, they are feeding the continuing house price spiral in a self-defeating cycle that cannot continue for ever.

THE RISE OF MORTGAGES
1930: 2 times annual salary, and 8% of annual income
2005: 4 times annual salary, and 20% of annual income

Michael Rowbotham
*The Grip of Death: A study of modern money,
debt slavery and destructive economics*
Jon Carpenter, 1998

Debt 1
Weighing down the world

"Nothing is more important to the poorest nations of Latin America and Africa than to be able to keep more of what they earn and invest it in their people, and the lives and well-being of their children."

Muhammad Ali, supporting the Jubilee 2000 campaign
to cancel poor countries' debts

Nearly all the money in circulation is there because it was borrowed, and that means that we are struggling under a monstrous weight of debt. That is true for us as individuals, as companies and as nations.

Corporations need to be seriously indebted just to protect themselves from hostile takeovers. If they have any spare borrowing capacity, the chances are that a corporate raider or hedge fund could use it to issue junk bonds with which to buy the company (see page 129). Then they are forced into ever more ambitious expansion plans just to pay off the interest on their loans.

Nobody knows the total of bad debts that now weigh down the world's banks, because few of them have come clean about it. But one estimate puts the total value of dodgy investments, including risky sub-prime loans, at as much as $45 trillion – twice the total value of the US stock market and three times the GDP of the United States.

As individuals, our unused borrowing capacity is the subject of serious marketing pressure. In the USA, some credit card companies market themselves by sending cheques for $5,000 through the post. The average adult American has been offered 32 credit cards, regardless of their credit history. All you have to do to open an account and spend the money is fill in your name – "like feeding lettuce to hungry rabbits", according to one American commentator.

The idea that high cost, high risk mortgages could be sold to those who could barely afford them, and then be bundled up into 'safe' investments, was precisely the cause of the 2007–8 credit crunch. The result is that millions of American homes are being repossessed, while the bankers responsible are often still drawing down bonuses.

But even without the banks, there are the loan sharks and money lenders, offering loans at outrageous rates of interest – sometimes up to as much as 5,000 per cent APR (see page 21). Meanwhile, personal debts are increasing at the rate of £1 million every five minutes.

Developing countries' debt is also a continuing scandal. The money was often lent by Western banks to ferocious military regimes that have since disappeared. Despite the debt cancellation of the past decade, the poorest 149 countries in the world still owe over \$2.6 trillion, most of it the result of mounting compound interest. The countries of sub-Saharan Africa pay \$10 billion every year in debt service, or about four times as much money as they spend on healthcare and education.

The debt all has to be repaid not in their own currencies, but in pounds or dollars, which these countries can only earn by converting forests or marginal land to grow cash crops for export like coffee. But worse still:

● The trickle of aid money from the rich North to the poor South is dwarfed by the enormous daily interest payments back again. The net flow of money is now about \$680 billion flowing from the poor to the rich every year.

● Even after the promises and hype, only about \$88 billion in debt has been written off. The rest still causes enormous hardship for the poorest people in the world.

● International loans are negotiated in secret between local élites and powerful creditors, but the effects are felt by ordinary people.

● As much as 95 per cent of debts owed to Britain are owed to the government's Export Credit Guarantee Department, which offered them as inducements to buy British exports – mainly arms.

● There is no international bankruptcy law to protect debtors and no international receiver: creditors act as judge and jury in their very own court room.

But then, who really owes whom?

● **Eco-debt:** Damage to the planet's eco-system is done by rich countries, but has its greatest effect on poor countries: 96 per cent of deaths from natural disasters are in poor countries, and seven million people are at risk from rising sea levels.

• **Imperial debt:** In the 150 years after Columbus, 185,000 kilograms of gold and 16 million kilograms of silver were taken from Central America to Europe. Was it theft or just a loan?

• **Historic debt:** In 1193, England agreed to pay Germany £66,000 in silver – then a quarter of their GDP – as ransom for Richard the Lionheart. It has never been completely paid. Some debts do get overtaken by history – or should that one be repaid too?

Some countries, of course, manage their loans better than others – and the right to credit is important. But the lender should be equally responsible for the original loan if they lent to the wrong people for the wrong reasons.

AVERAGE HOUSEHOLD DEBT IN THE UK:

1997	£24,500
2003	£37,500
2007	£56,600

www.jubileedebtcampaign.org.uk

Debt 2
Weighing down the USA

"280 million Americans bingeing on Toyota Land Cruisers, Sony video players and Cartier watches – are doing so by raiding the piggy bank savings of five billion people in developing countries. It's time the rich financed the poor, instead of filching from them."

Ann Pettifor, *Advocacy International*, 2006

Just around the corner from Times Square in New York City there is a rapidly spinning counter that shows the USA debt. It is now running at $9,524,400,933,800, which means over $31,000 per person – and increasing at the rate of $1.74 billion a day.

Local government in the USA has also been on a spending binge and now owes $2,000 billion, paying more in interest payments than they are on parks, libraries and recreation combined – and all to be paid off by later generations.

The USA used to be the world's creditor nation. It forced the British to restructure their economy after World War I and it is a creditor to many of the poorest countries. But it is also now massively in debt itself to the rest of the world.

Every day, the US government finances itself by selling Treasury bonds and Treasury bills, paying a set amount of interest, to whoever has money to lend. When the bonds and bills become due, it borrows more to pay them, as well as to pay the cost of arms, tax cuts and all the rest of their unsustainable budget, which ballooned during Ronald Reagan's presidency (1981–9). Its budgets were balanced again in the Clinton years (1993–2001) but unbalanced again by George W Bush's tax cuts and military adventures (2001–8). The US debt now hoovers up most of the available money in the world.

Ironically, it is the savers, pension funds and central banks in the poorer countries, as well as countries with a trade surplus – like France, Germany and China – who keep the money flowing. The world trusts the United States to pay its debts, and no creditor so far has dared demand that it restructure itself, though China – which has been increasing its share of American debt at the rate of $18 billion a month – has the 'nuclear' option of selling it off, threatening a collapse in the value of the dollar and high inflation in the USA.

Experts are divided about what this means: can it just continue or will there be some bizarre crack in the world's financial architecture? Nobody knows, but the ironies are very peculiar:

• The USA alone owes more than the whole developing world put together, including India, China and Brazil.
• The USA pays only $20 billion a year to service its debt, while poor countries are crippled by more than $300 billion servicing the same amount, because they are considered to be greater risks.
• Poor countries borrow funds from the USA at interest rates as high as 18 per cent per year, while at the same time lending to the USA at rates as low as just three per cent.
• The developing countries are actually financing the USA's massive deficits, partly because of the hoover effect and partly because their central banks are forced to hold dollar reserves as insurance against speculation and financial instability.

But then, who knows, the poorest nations may yet wake up to their unexpectedly powerful position. The fear is that forcing the USA to restructure its debts could have devastating consequences for the rest of the world.

HOUSEHOLD DEBT IN THE USA DURING THE BOOM YEARS:

2001	**$8 trillion**
2008	**$14 trillion**

Ann Pettifor
The Coming First World Debt Crisis
Palgrave Macmillan, 2006

Where has all the money gone?
The problem with modern money

"The plain fact is that a man, and his wife, and with four children that are unable to work, cannot now, out of his labour, possibly provide them and himself with the means for living … And will anyone say that this state of things is such as England ought to witness?"

William Cobbett, *Paper against Gold*, 1817

My parents live in a little village called Nether Wallop. A generation ago it had two shops, a post office, two pubs, a butcher, a policeman, a doctor and district nurse, and a nearby railway station – connected to a massive local rail network. And that was in the 'austerity' years of the 1940s. Now, when we are incomparably 'richer', all that's left is one pub and a very occasional bus. The conventional reasons for this – low taxes, over-regulation, fat-cat salaries – do not really explain why it is so hard to afford the simplest public services, health, post and education any more, or basic shops.

Policy-makers have their noses glued to the short term, and find it hard to ask long-term questions. But an increasingly urgent question is: why can we only afford a creaking postal system that occasionally delivers letters within 24 hours, and barely adequate railways? Or why – for example – do restaurants have to be almost fully booked just to avoid bankruptcy? Why can't we afford to clean the streets or litter from the parks? Why can't we afford care for the mentally ill?

Victorian economists worked out that in 1495, peasants had to work at least 15 weeks a year to earn the money they needed to survive. By 1564 it was 40 weeks. Now it is impossible for one person on an average wage to buy a home in south-east England and live reasonably in it: that requires two salaries.

The 20th century predictions that we would all soon relax into a leisured life, fuelled by technology and the effects of compound interest, have not come true. Some flaw in the economic system has conspired to turn us instead into slaves to our mortgages.

Why does the system work like that? There is no definitive answer, and most economists don't even ask the question, but here are some possible reasons:

• **Burgeoning debt:** At least a third of the price of the goods we pay, or the rooms we rent, goes on interest payments to cover the money borrowed. An average 28 per cent of UK business income goes to service debt.

• **Offshore tax havens:** Britain loses between £25 billion and £80 billion a year in lost corporation tax, the tax on profits that companies have to pay. British companies can avoid it by registering in tax havens where they pay minimal tax (see page 54).

• **The curse of the middlemen:** Half a century ago, American farmers used to get 41 cents of every dollar spent on the food they grew. Now they get just 9 cents, with 24 cents going on seeds, energy, fertiliser and other inputs, and 67 cents going to marketeers, middlemen, transport and supermarkets.

• **Intellectual property:** The ultra-rich now siphon off much of the available money in the world, either through interest payments, copyrights or intellectual property or through rents – taking rights over other people's money, media, manufactures or homes (see page 56).

• **Monopolies:** A handful of companies now dominate the markets in grain, seeds, groceries and a range of other products, and can control many aspects of the price.

Whatever the reason, the trend is clear: we are turning ourselves into economic slaves – and creating a world where the public 'good' seems more and more unaffordable. What can we do about it?

• We can find new ways of creating a range of new kinds of money that are locally controlled (see page 167).

• We can persuade the government to start issuing its own interest-free money – put into circulation, rather than borrowed into existence with interest attached, as it usually is (see page 98).

• We can break up the monopolies (see page 31).

We can also limit the ownership rights of investors. If investors never look beyond 20 years when they buy foreign companies or build foreign factories – and they don't – then we are overpaying them by giving them perpetual rights.

Australian former financier Shann Turnbull suggests that rights should revert to locals after one generation (see page 58).

Most of all, we should be aware of what is happening. Ordinary people are increasingly indebted, public bodies are increasingly cash-strapped, and governments are increasingly penniless. Corporations are increasingly wealthy, but so dependent on the tyranny of the stock markets and their own share price that they dare not step out of line. Between them, the money that allows us to live is being allowed to slip away.

Number of food shops in the UK (1950):   221,662
Number of food shops in the UK (1997):   36,931

David Boyle (editor)
The Money Changers: Currency reform from Aristotle to e-cash
Earthscan, 2002

Pensions
One thing after another

"This was a massive debacle. We just hope it never happens again."
Malcolm McLean, UK Pensions Advisory Service
on the most recent pensions scandal

A century ago, music hall audiences would dab their eyes at the end of the song 'My Old Dutch': "We've been together now for 40 years, And it don't seem a day too much" – watching the elderly couple separate forever into the Men's and Women's entrances of the workhouse.

We no longer have to face that prospect, partly because of state pensions, introduced by David Lloyd George in his People's Budget of 1909, which began to sweep away the workhouses. And partly because of the effects of compound interest – the 'original sin' at the heart of the money system – which allows people to build up enough savings to see them through their retirement. There was a time when employees would pay regularly into their company pension scheme every week, and – thanks to the magical effects of compound interest – they would be rewarded with maybe three decades of happy workhouse-free, comfortable retirement.

But that has all begun to unravel. This is partly because endless money growth is unsustainable – the planet doesn't work like that (see page 83) – and partly because of the simultaneous collapse of the stock market and interest rates. Also we have an ageing population and falling savings rates. So we are faced again with the return of the spectre of poverty-stricken old age, thanks to the incompetence, arrogance and corporate greed that has undermined confidence in financial services on both sides of the Atlantic. Recent pension scandals include:

• **The Savings and Loans Scandal:** When building societies in the USA (known as 'savings and loans') were deregulated in the mid-1980s, they were allowed to lend their own owners money. The result was an explosion of greed, corruption and political slush-funds that amounted to the largest theft in the history of the world – implicating Republicans at the highest level – and cost an estimated $1,400 billion. That would have been enough to provide pre-natal care for every American child for 2,300 years. The few who went to jail received sentences on average a fifth that of the average bank robber.

• **The Maxwell Scandal:** When he fell off his yacht in the Bay of Biscay in 1991, the publishing tycoon Robert Maxwell turned out to have been plundering the pensions of his Mirror Publishing Group. Workers who had saved for years received reduced pensions as a result. Several years on, none of the highly paid professionals who were supposed to be taking responsibility for the security of the pension fund have been punished.

• **The Pensions Mis-selling Scandal:** Up to two million UK customers were mis-sold personal pensions and pension top-ups in the late 1980s, and persuaded to opt out of company schemes that would have been far more beneficial. The scandal looks set to cost insurers and financial advisers at least £11.8 billion in compensation payments. The UK's financial services watchdog took disciplinary action against as many as 346 firms.

• **The Company Pensions Scandal:** Most companies are backing off their commitments to look after staff in old age, with only a handful of final-salary schemes still open to new members. They are being replaced by so-called 'money purchase' schemes, which do not guarantee the level of pension on retirement. They also cost the company less.

• **The Privatisation Scandal:** In 1988 the privatised National Bus Company was sold off by the Conservative government, which then allowed its pension fund surplus to be counted as an asset of the privatised company, benefiting shareholders rather than the staff who had paid for it. There were many other privatisation scandals like it.

• **The Winding-up Scandal:** By the end of the 1990s, employees who had paid into company schemes for decades increasingly found themselves without pensions because of board decisions to wind-up the company. Worse, they had to watch while up to 15 per cent of some pension funds disappeared into the pockets of lawyers, actuaries and professional trustees during the wind-up process.

• **The Public Sector Pensions Scandal:** The UK government pays its former employees' pensions out of the current account, but has studiously refrained from working out what it might cost in the future.

The latest estimate is £800 billion, and index-linked as well, to pay the pensions of the NHS, teachers and the armed forces. They will not be able to pay it without planning ahead, and that they fail to do.

What can we do about all this? State pensions should, properly, be for a living income: we need to reconnect them to average earnings. And private pension funds have got to find something more reliable to invest in than the global casino – such as safe and productive havens like local housing, transport or health projects.

We probably need to raise the retirement age from 65, the age chosen originally in Germany by Bismarck as when most public pensioners would be dead. It is a kind of lie to carry on pretending that people over 60 and 65 are no longer willing or able to work: in fact the reverse is usually the case.

We also need to find new ways of safeguarding ourselves in old age – making sure there is a supportive community around us to keep us healthy and at home. This is one of the reasons time banks were first introduced, as a way of reconnecting people with each other in a supportive way (see page 186).

The UK pensions gap (the gap between what we will need and what we have):   £130 billion

Lisa H Newton
Permission to Steal: Revealing the roots of corporate scandal
Blackwell Publishing, 2006

Another way of making money 1
Creating more cash

"If the government can create a dollar bond, they can create a dollar bill."
Henry Ford, *New York Times*, 1921

What can we do about the dwindling supply of money for some key sectors, cities and public projects? There is a renewed argument emerging that it should be created interest-free by the government, and then lent to public projects. Once these have paid it back, this money should be withdrawn from circulation. This system would replace the current arrangement, where projects borrow money from commercial banks (who create it) and then pay back plus interest.

This was a popular radical solution in the mid-20th century, when the leading economist Irving Fisher urged a ban on banks creating money. If they lent money, he argued, they should only lend what had been deposited with them and nothing more. It was an early proposal by what became the Chicago School of Economists (see page 36).

The solution of creating the money interest-free and then, when it was paid back, withdrawing it from circulation, was proposed in 1921 by the industrialists Henry Ford and Thomas Alva Edison as a way of paying for the building of dams.

If the money has to be created anyway, it might be less inflationary if it were created by the government without interest than by the banks. Economists say that interest is a discipline on big loans and that is true. But it is an expensive discipline on public projects: investors in the London Underground expected to make about £2.7 billion over the life of the ill-fated Public–Private Partnership, in return for investments of just £530 million – and a third of that went to financial intermediaries. There are precedents for money created in this way:

• **Bradburys:** In 1914, Chancellor of the Exchequer David Lloyd George staved off a banking collapse by getting the Treasury to print their own bank notes, known as 'bradburys' because they were signed by the Treasury Secretary Sir John Bradbury. The banks were furious when it continued.

• **Cash:** About three per cent of the money in circulation is created in this way already – and it used to be much more. These are the notes and coins the government issues, making a profit known as 'seignorage' – the difference between what it costs to print notes and their face value.

The American experience of issuing 'greenbacks' during the Civil War suggests that governments creating too much money can cause inflation. But as recently as 1960, about 21 per cent of the money in circulation in the UK was issued by the Bank of England as cash, and inflation was the same as it is today – so there must be scope to do the same now to create the credit needed for civilised investments.

Astonishingly, the financial crisis became so bad in the UK by 2009 that the Bank of England began creating money in just this way, calling it 'quantitative easing'. They put money into circulation by buying assets, often government bonds, from banks and financial service companies. The problem is that this is rather indirect: giving more money to banks in the often vain hope that they will lend it on somewhere useful, when the money could have been used directly for something useful in the first place.

Amount of money circulating in the UK that is created by banks: 97%

Amount of money circulating in the UK that is created by the government in interest-free notes and coins: 3%

James Robertson and Joseph Huber
Creating New Money: A monetary reform for the information age
New Economics Foundation, 2000

Another way of making money 2
Social credit and the rise of the Greenshirts

"Banking was conceived in iniquity and born in sin … Bankers own the earth. Take it away from them but leave them the power to create money, and with a flick of the pen, they will create enough money to buy it back again."

Sir Josiah Stamp, Bank of England director, attributed to a speech he made to the University of Texas in 1927

In the turbulent 1920s and 1930s, the idea of the government creating new money became the central belief of a new ideology – arising out of an amalgam of socialism and enthusiasm for the days of medieval guilds – known as social credit. The founder of this ideology, 'Major' Clifford Hugh Douglas, was an engineer at the Farnborough aircraft factories. "There isn't enough money in circulation to pay off all the debts in the world," he said, "so our lives are bound to slip further and further into the control of the banks." And this is still so today.

Douglas's 1920 book *Economic Democracy* caused a major division on the political Left, and – although it was never quite clear what Douglas wanted to do about the situation – a powerful manifesto was to grow up around him.

It included banning the banks from creating money altogether, so they could only lend what someone had deposited with them, and creating money in the form of a basic income for every citizen, credited to their account every month, which would 'trickle up' the economy rather than 'trickle down' as wealth was usually supposed to do.

By the 1930s, Douglas was able to command huge stadiums full of supporters in Australia and Canada, as well as in the UK. An estimated 90 million tuned into his radio broadcasts in the USA, and two Canadian states elected social credit administrations. They stayed in power in Alberta until 1971, prevented by the courts from pushing through their promised $25 dividend per person a month.

In the UK, a breakaway wing of the Boy Scouts known as Kibbo Kift formed itself into the Social Credit Party – much to Douglas's horror – and marched in green uniform as the Greenshirts. The extraordinary man behind it, John Hargrave, became a notorious figure just before World War II when a green arrow was fired into the door of 10 Downing Street. But when he lost his deposit as a candidate for Stoke Newington in the 1950 general election, he wound the party up.

The social credit campaign petered out in paranoia and anti-Semitism in the 1950s: for some reason, those who believe there is a conspiracy of bankers seem to be only a hair's-breadth away from believing it is a Jewish one. The conspiracies are still there on the internet: both Lincoln and Kennedy are supposed to have been assassinated because they were poised to take on the banks.

But Douglas influenced young economists like James Meade, who claimed Keynes had learned from him too. Now, half a century later, social credit has shaken off its anti-Semitism and is back in vogue as a radical solution to the world debt crisis. But it is still controversial because it would hand power over the money supply to the centre, whether it is the government or to a few establishment figures around a table.

Governments have always been notorious for their uncertainty over how much money to issue, but even an 'independent' board is a centralising force. This is the stuff of radical debate: the present system doesn't work, but do we concentrate money – creating power at the centre – or do we widen the number of institutions able to create money, or both?

SOCIAL CREDIT ELECTORAL VICTORIES
Alberta (Canada) 1935 (stayed in power until 1971)
British Columbia (Canada) 1952

Frances Hutchinson
What Everybody Really Wants to Know about Money
Jon Carpenter, 1998

Another way of making money 3
A new global currency of oil, metal and food ...

"We have had no reality, no stability. The price of gold has risen by more than 70 per cent. That is as if a 12-inch foot rule had suddenly stretched to 19 or 20 inches."

Winston Churchill, on his disastrous decision to return the pound to the Gold Standard, speech to House of Commons, 1931

What can we do about the dwindling supply of money for some vital aspects of life? Other traditions of monetary reform stress not so much the lack of money in the system, but the problem that money is no longer based on anything, and has become a commodity in its own right.

Leaving the Gold Standard behind in 1931 was overwhelmingly positive, but if money isn't based on the value of anything, it can be worth whatever people in Wall Street say it is – and that really can be anything. There is always somewhere more profitable for money to be lodged than in growing or making something. So it is hardly surprising that it slips effortlessly out of the hands of small farmers or manufacturers and into the hands of banks, hedge funds, financial services and the mega-rich.

That is what happens when the vast majority of money in the world is 'fiat' money (money that has value because governments say it does, see page 40). These currencies exist just because their governments say they exist, and their value is underpinned by debt – by what the governments borrowed to create it and by confidence in their ability to repay it.

But there is a long tradition that demands something different – from the French anarchist Pierre-Joseph Proudhon and his 1848 People's Bank (see page 178), who wanted money based on the value of goods and services, to the American conscientious objector Bob Swann, who invented money based on farm produce in the 1990s. They include

Keynes, whose plan for the economic system after World War II – vetoed by the American government – included an international currency that would underpin everything else and was based on commodities like wheat or oil. This kind of stability was urgent during the post-war famine years in Europe. The grand old man of investment banking, Benjamin Graham, proposed a global currency based on the value of food kept in stores around the world.

Most recent is the plan by one of the original designers of the euro, Bernard Lietaer, for the 'terra' – a world currency, based on a basket of commodities (anything from copper to sugar), that would keep all the other currencies, national and local, but complement and support them. It would be inflation-free, but like real commodities it would 'corrode' when it was stored: it would carry a small charge for holding it – a negative interest rate – to promote sustainability.

BERNARD LIETAER'S EXAMPLES (2001) OF HOW TO PRICE THE TERRA:
1 tenth of a barrel of oil
1 bushel of wheat
2 pounds of copper
1 hundredth of an ounce of gold

Bernard Lietaer
The Future of Money: A new way to create wealth, work and a wiser world
Century, 2001

Another way of making money 4
Citizens' income

"A feast is made for laughter, and wine maketh merry; but money answereth all things."

Ecclesiastes 10:19

Vast bureaucracies spend enormous sums of money every year trying to make sure that nobody gets unemployment benefits, or any other kind of pay-out, unless they really need them. You can't help wondering whether it would be cheaper just to give them to everyone.

When you think how easy it is to earn a living doing jobs of no possible use to people or planet (like writing tobacco adverts, or flipping burgers in a fast-food restaurant), and how difficult it is to get paid to do jobs that aren't valued in the market (childcare, looking after the environment), you have to wonder whether it might be better to cut the link between jobs and basic income altogether. People could then earn extra money for luxuries, but – if they wanted just to devote their life to art, or looking after their elderly parents – they could do so.

Citizens' income means a basic income, on which people could survive, paid to individuals as of right by the government. They would need to work to have enough money to do anything beyond surviving. It was one of the ideas behind the social credit movement in the 1930s (see page 100), though the Canadian supreme court prevented the social credit government in Alberta in 1935 from paying everyone a 'dividend' every month.

In the UK, a minority report to the Beveridge plan for the welfare state in 1943 proposed something similar, but paid for out of taxation. Tax credits for families are also a slow movement towards a basic citizens' income – making sure every individual has enough to live on – but they add to the bureaucracy, rather than reducing it.

The idea still has some way to go before it is accepted – as paying for a citizen's income through taxation would require huge increases.

Opinions differ about what it would cost. There are other pitfalls too: employers would be tempted to lower wages, knowing that the state was taking over their responsibility. It might lower some people's self-esteem, because they wouldn't be forced to go out to earn – which is a life-saver for some people. But even so, the benefits of a citizens' income could be enormous. It would mean, for example:

• No more means testing, no more bullying unemployment benefits officials, no vast welfare bureaucracy, because everyone would have money to live on – as of right.
• No more trapping artists, actors, poets and others in inappropriate jobs just to make ends meet.
• No more chasing after the very people who keep neighbourhoods running – spending their time looking out for people, supporting the elderly, building social capital – to force them out to look for 'paid' work.
• No more of the nonsense where people can be paid to look after the children next door, but not for looking after their own.
• No more low wages for vital jobs like nurses and care workers – they would have to be increased to attract people into these jobs.

There may be other ways to pay for the citizens' income too. Norway invests its oil revenues into a fund that will benefit future generations. And if foreign investments reverted to local ownership after 20 years (see page 58), people could be paid an annual dividend every year from the profits.

The current system now defines what a job is increasingly narrowly, and it impoverishes us all by driving out everything that isn't immediately marketable. Unless we have citizens' incomes, of course.

Amount paid out to each man, woman and child in Alaska by the Alaska Permanent Fund in 2005: $845

www.citizensincome.org

Another way of making money 5
Small-scale banking

"In the future the question will not be, 'Are people credit-worthy', but rather, 'Are banks people-worthy?'"

Muhammad Yunus, founder of the Grameen Bank, 1976

Economics professor Muhammad Yunus was at a conference of New York bankers in 1976 when he realised that at least 80 per cent of his fellow Bangladeshis would be turned down for loans by the bankers in the room.

He went home and founded the Grameen Bank, now the model for micro-lending and small-scale banking all over the world. It lends very small amounts – enough for a hen or a cow, or, more recently, a mobile phone that can be used by a whole village ("a mobile phone is a cow" they say at Grameen). The money is lent almost entirely to women, because they were found to manage money better than men, and each loan is rooted in support groups of other women.

Grameen originally operated from motor-scooters, around some of the poorest villages in the world. "Your bank just rushed past in a cloud of dust", said the headline of the first article about them, in *Christian Science Monitor* in 1987.

It was also enormously successful. They reduced bad debts to a tiny amount compared to Western banks lending to rich people, but they also set out a whole new model of development that could genuinely help the poorest people stay independent. They now have a presence in 35,000 villages in Bangladesh, with 12,000 workers and two million borrowers – 94 per cent of whom are women – and they have serious political clout. Grameen also provides the investment people and small businesses need to make a major difference to people's lives, by providing services or food to neighbours in the poorest places – rather than waiting hopelessly for big corporations to provide anything along the same lines.

Grameen has spawned thousands of micro-credit projects all over the world, and is one of the ways that the developed world is learning about development from the developing world:

• **Credit unions:** These are already well established in Ireland and the USA and are now expanding rapidly in the UK, as people lose faith in the big banks. (Two million people are still denied a conventional bank account in the UK.)

• **Community development banks:** like the London Rebuilding Society and the Aston Reinvestment Trust. This new kind of bank was targeted for expansion in the USA by Bill Clinton, since when American credit unions have attracted over one million low and moderate income members, mobilising savings of over $4 billion and advancing new loans of over $3 billion a year.

• **Community banking partnerships:** a co-operative link-up between credit unions, community development finance institutions and money advice agencies. Seven of these partnerships are operating in East London, mid-Wales, Coventry and Warwickshire, Devon, Portsmouth and Southampton, Merseyside and Sheffield.

FAIR FINANCE
(Community banking partnership in east London) has:
Stopped 100 evictions
Rescheduled £500,000 of household debt
Provided over 400 micro-loans a year to households otherwise paying 160% plus interest rates.

Muhammad Yunus
The autobiography of Muhammad Yunus, founder of the Grameen Bank
Aurum Press, 1998

Green New Deal
A new way forward

"Practical men, who believe themselves to be quite exempt from any intellectual influence, are usually the slaves of some defunct economist."
John Maynard Keynes,
General Theory of Employment, Interest and Money, 1936

In 2008, the so-called credit crunch (see page 133) brought to a head the combination of climate crunch, energy crunch and food crunch. When conventional economists faced the unprecedented conditions of the Great Depression in the 1930s, they only had their old meagre tools to fall back on. It took Roosevelt's New Deal, borrowing ideas from Keynes (see page 34) and Lloyd George, to drag the USA through and into better times.

The similarity with today was obvious to a group of green economists, including the *Guardian*'s economics editor (Larry Elliott), two former Friends of the Earth directors (Tony Juniper and Charles Secrett), leading green campaigners (Colin Hines, Andrew Simms and Ann Pettifor) and others, who hammered out a proposal for a Green New Deal capable of tackling the 'Triple Crunch' that lay before us. Published in August 2008, it is still the most important proposal for concerted emergency action.

They came up with a set of emergency solutions that could rein in the reckless finance sector and make a real difference to people – with massive investment in sustainable energy, green-collar jobs and low-cost capital. The next task is to build a political coalition around it, or at least something along similar lines.

After all, when confidence in money collapses, what do we do to drag the economy back from the brink without damaging our chances of sound economics long-term – and build a greener economy at the same time? If the Transition Towns movement (see page 162) is the local solution, the Green New Deal is a potential national one. It urges the government to:

• Execute a bold low-carbon energy system that will include making 'every building a power station'.

- Create and train a 'carbon army' of workers to provide the human resources for a vast environmental reconstruction programme.
- Set up an Oil Legacy Fund, paid for by a windfall tax on the profits of oil and gas companies, plus local authority green bonds, green gilts and green family savings bonds.
- Make sure fossil fuel prices include the cost to the environment, and are high enough to tackle climate change by creating economic incentives to drive efficiently and bring alternative fuels to market.
- Minimise corporate tax avoidance by clamping down on tax havens and corporate financial reporting, deducting tax at source for all income paid to financial institutions in tax havens.
- Re-regulate the domestic financial system, cutting interest rates – including the Bank of England's rate – and changing debt-management policy to enable reductions in interest rates across all government borrowing (the interest rates were cut massively soon afterwards).
- Break up the financial institutions that have needed so much public money to prop them up in the latest credit crunch, de-merging large banking and finance groups and splitting retail banking from both corporate finance and securities dealing.

Most are now on the mainstream political agenda. The publication of the Green New Deal was followed by a flurry of other 'green new deals', one launched by the United Nations, another urged by the UK Environment Agency, and there are signs that all political parties have learned from aspects of the original. The Green New Deal was certainly a success; it remains to be seen how much it will actually be put into practice.

President Bush's first bail-out of the banks: $700 billion

A Green New Deal: Joined-up policies to solve the triple crunch of the credit crisis, climate change and high oil prices
New Economics Foundation, 2008

Mad money

The world's financial system creates new billionaires every day, presides over grinding poverty and debt, and is increasingly unstable – and among the people who run it are 24-year-olds in braces in London and New York who make more money the more it fluctuates. It's a crazy world out there …

Criminal money
The shadow economy

"I am just a businessman."

Al Capone, American gangster in the 1920s and '30s

One of the peculiar attributes of money is that throughout history, it has tended to drive out entrenched privilege. Medieval rulers watched in horror as merchants affected equality with them simply because they had money. So they hurriedly drafted rules about what people of different classes could wear, even banning non-aristocrats from playing chess, because of the risk that they might win. But it all got swept away: that was the power of money. It has an aristocracy of its own, but it destroys any other.

But money now devours anything that gets in the way – family, morality, community, laws – with terrifying rapidity. The result is that the biggest industries in the world, apart from oil and arms, are now drugs, sex and illegal immigration.

The annual profits from drug trafficking (cannabis, cocaine, heroin) are estimated at over $300 billion, which is getting on for ten per cent of all world trade. Even software piracy has a turnover of more than $200 billion, with counterfeit goods – all those pirated CDs and DVDs – at around $100 billion. The more copyrights and patents spread, the more delighted the 'underworld' will be.

The world turnover of crime every year – the Gross Criminal Product – is now believed to run at around $1,000 billion, or about 20 per cent of world trade. Of that, about $350 billion annually is laundered through offshore financial centres and reinvested – that's about $1 billion a day.

Some of the activities of legitimate corporations could be included in the 'criminal' class. About 56,000 Americans die every year at work or from occupational diseases such as black lung and asbestosis. Hundreds of thousands of people all over the world also succumb to the silent violence of pollution, contaminated foods, hazardous consumer products, and hospital malpractice. Except when companies cause actionable damage – children born deformed because of chemicals used to grow tobacco, for example – economists call these negative impacts 'externalities'.

The top companies with 'criminal records' in recent years have been:

• Swiss drugs firm Hoffmann-La Roche, fined $500 million under international antitrust regulations (1999).
• Bernard Madoff, whose investment scheme may amount to the biggest investment fraud by a single person – $50 billion (2009).
• Exxon Corporation and Exxon Shipping, fined $125 million for pollution after the *Exxon Valdez* disaster (1989).
• Enron, which defrauded about $11 billion from the two states of Washington and California alone, by overstating energy demand to force unfair settlements on the state governments (2001).
• Worldcom, responsible for the biggest accounting fraud in corporate history, boosting their reported earnings by six per cent to meet Wall Street targets (2001).

Nor are shadowy executive pay deals always quite the wholly legal business they seem. The CEO of the US conglomerate Tyco, Dennis Kozlowski, and his finance chief Mark Swartz, were charged in 2003 with pilfering $400 million from company coffers over ten years. Kozlowski had a penchant for $6,000 shower curtains and $15,000 umbrella stands.

But this type of behaviour is hardly surprising when policy-makers assume that the only moral duty on business is to make a profit. The trick has to be to find a new model for business, and a new design for the short-termism built into the financial markets.

TRANSCRIPT OF TAPES SEIZED FROM ENRON IN 2001
EXECUTIVE 1: "It's called lies. It's all how well you can weave these lies together, Shari, alright, so."
EXECUTIVE 2: "I feel like I'm being corrupted now."
EXECUTIVE 1: "No, this is marketing."

www.corporatepredators.org

The curse of oil
Why nothing is real any more

*"The Stone Age came to an end not for a lack of stones; the oil age will end,
but not for a lack of oil."*

Sheik Yamani, former oil minister of Saudi Arabia,
Daily Telegraph, 19 June 2001

"What makes her poor is her wealth," said a 16th-century Spanish
economist about Spain, awash with gold and struggling with the effects
of crippling inflation as a result. A similar disaster overtook Peru during
the guano boom (to 1870) and Brazil during the rubber boom (to 1920).
This paradox is the basis of the so-called 'curse of oil'.

Nothing excites governments more than suddenly discovering, as
the British did in the 1960s, that they have oil on their back doorsteps.
The rush of black gold from the seabed or deep in the Earth is enough
to make the owners of the rights believe that their troubles are over
once and for all. Actually the opposite is true, which is why Juan Pablo
Perez Alfonzo, the former Venezuelan oil minister and co-founder of the
petroleum-producing club OPEC, called oil 'the devil's excrement'.

There are exceptions to the rule, like Norway and Malaysia who
have used their oil revenues to diversify their economies. But generally
speaking, the countries that are most dependent on oil wealth do worse
over time, and the countries least dependent on it do best. Strange, isn't it?

Why should that be? What comes easy also goes easy: booms end,
leaving behind some gaudy buildings crumbling away, or ghost towns –
all that is left of the gold rushes in California and Alaska. Meanwhile,
the brief cascade of money has encouraged the beneficiaries to spend,
spend, spend without much thought for the future – which always
arrives in the end.

Booms also drive out the most useful people. If you doubt it, have a
look at the small town of Black Hawk after the legalisation of gambling
in Colorado, where almost every public building has become a casino or
slot machine arcade, and the only people on the streets are men in dark
glasses offering to park your car. A similar process is under way on a

grander scale in offshore financial centres like Jersey, where agriculture is barely viable, tourism is struggling, and only financial services can afford to play a key role in the island's economy.

Oil lulls nations into a false sense of security. They believe the wealth will cushion them against the need for tough decisions and investment. They believe energy will always be cheap – the belief that has crippled the USA – which means they never have to innovate to save energy.

Or if you are really unlucky, oil-rich nations end up like the Niger delta, where oil was first discovered in 1956. Half a century on, the land and air are hideously polluted, the profits are still being siphoned off by politicians, violence and crime is everywhere, and the local young people are trapped into an unproductive get-rich-quick mentality, desperate to get into the corrupt business of local oil at whatever cost.

The UK's own version of the curse of oil affects other countries too: oil wealth feeds into wages and prices, and – worst of all – boosts the value of your currency in world markets, as speculators buy into it for a brief period. The eventual result is that people around the world can no longer afford your products, and your factories start closing one by one, as they did in the UK during the peak oil production period in the 1980s.

That is the curse of oil: all your economy is left with is oil and financial services. Manufacturing gets priced out, and anyway, why start a business – with all that effort and those low margins – when you can simply share in the spoils of the stock market bubbles?

HOW TO DO IT RIGHT
Citizen funds, saved from oil revenue savings on behalf of the citizens:
Assets of the Norwegian Petroleum Fund: $150 billion
Assets of the Alaska Permanent Fund: $28 billion

Terry Lynn Karl
The Paradox of Plenty: Oil booms and petro-states
University of California Press, 1997

Goodbye real world
Money as a commodity

"While a bushel of corn sold for less than $4, a bushel of corn flakes sold for $133."

Canadian National Farmers Union report, 2000

About two centuries have gone by since the Industrial Revolution, and more than half a century since policy-makers started staring at the dial showing economic 'growth' – but one thing never changes. No matter how much success the economy seems to produce, no matter how much production, the gulf between the rich and poor remains – and grows.

When the shipping magnate Charles Booth organised the first door-to-door survey of London in the 1880s, to win a bet, he discovered that 30.5 per cent of Londoners were 'poor'. Even further back, before the New Poor Law Amendment Act of 1834 introduced workhouses, just over 20 per cent of national income in the UK was spent on welfare.

Now in the 21st century we measure these things differently, but both have remained broadly the same: about a third of UK cities are poor, just as a third of nations are considered 'Less Developed Countries'.

But now it is more complicated than that – and much worse. Money favours the already rich over the poor, and already rich countries over poor ones. The unreal economy of financial services also favours speculation over the people who make things, just as it favours the people who know things over the people who grow things (see page 56). It favours hard-edged pseudo-scientific skills – such as accountancy – over human skills like nursing and caring.

Of all the money insanities in history, the commodification of money is the most insidious, the most damaging and the most unfair. Why does it happen? The problem is the three Ms:

• **Monopolies:** Some corporations are in a semi-monopolistic position (see page 31). They squeeze those who rely on them – and are rewarded with a higher share price when they do – and none more so than the small farmers who are the backbone of any country's real production.

• **Middlemen:** Middlemen siphon off the money. Manufacturers, in particular, have lost out to powerful intermediaries – supermarkets, marketeers, advertisers. Packagers transform a pair of jeans made for 20 US cents each – sewed by women in Nicaragua often working 24-hour shifts, sleeping in cramped breeze-block rooms – into fashion items that sell in New York or London for $30.

• **Money:** No commodity can compete with money itself, which offers far bigger returns – to people who have access to almost infinite credit – than the small returns offered by any natural process. We therefore demand high returns – and are threatened with economic disaster when this inexorable growth starts to slide.

Commodity prices tend to recover in times of economic uncertainty, but when the economy recovers, so does the ratcheting of economic power away from those who produce the raw materials and grow the food. The result of this money insanity is all around us: identikit towns and high streets, identikit culture, increasing dependence on large corporations and, all over the world, bankrupt farms and suicidal farmers – like those in India who are too indebted to multinational seed companies and loan sharks to see any kind of future worth living.

RATE OF FINANCIAL GROWTH **1990–2006**
(despite which poverty remains much the same)

World GDP	× 2
World trade	× 3
World financial assets	× 4
World cross-border investment assets	× 5
World net financial flows	× 8

Vandana Shiva
Stolen Harvest: The hijacking of the global food supply
South End Press, 2000

Abstractions
Towards post-autistic economics

"Where is the wisdom we have lost in knowledge?
Where is the knowledge we have lost in information?"
TS Eliot, The Rock, 1934

Our society values hard numerical skills, although numbers are incapable of summing up the complexity of human truth. Meanwhile, soft human skills are down-valued. That is our tragedy and the source of so many of our basic inefficiencies and mistakes.

Of all the disciplines thus impoverished, economics has suffered the most. What began as a moral philosophy that tried to make sense of the way money behaves, has become a peculiar abstract business of formulae and statistics that bear little relation to the real world. Everyone knows that human beings don't actually pursue their own self-interest at all times, but – although many economists recognise this – economics formulae usually assume that most people do.

The result of this tyranny of numbers over truth is a kind of autism, according to a group of French economics students who launched the Post-Autistic Economics campaign in 2000.

"It was in the beginning a modest initiative, almost confidential," wrote the French newspaper *Le Monde* in September 2000. "It has now become a subject of an important debate which has created a state of effervescence in the community of economists. Should not the teaching of economics in universities be re-thought?"

A small group of students had protested on the web against the 'uncontrolled use of mathematics' in economics. They claimed that mathematics had 'become an end in itself', turning economics into what they called an 'autistic science', dominated by abstractions that bore no relation to the real world.

Within two weeks, the petition calling for reconnection with the real world had 150 signatures, many from France's most important universities. Soon newspapers and TV stations across France had picked up the story and senior professors were starting a similar petition of their

own. By the autumn, the campaign had led to a major debate at the
Sorbonne and the French education minister, Jack Lang, had promised
to set up a commission to investigate the situation and come up with
some proposals to change economics teaching.

By then, there had also been a vitriolic exchange of articles by
French and American economists, a counter-petition launched by the
Massachusetts Institute of Technology (MIT), and a peculiar Post-Autistic
petition from Cambridge PhD students – unusual in that the signatories
were too scared for their future careers to put their real names to it.

The Post-Autistic Economics movement has so far failed to
create a widespread public debate, but it has created the first dent
in the previously unassailable idea that people's individual and very
human behaviour patterns could somehow be summed up in a set of
mathematical equations.

POST-AUTISTIC ECONOMICS SIGNATORIES
To the Sorbonne petition, Paris	**797**
To the University of Missouri petition, Kansas City	**267**
To the Cambridge University petition	**27 (unnamed)**

www.paecon.net

Forgery
The scourge of fake money

"There wouldn't be such a thing as counterfeit gold if there were no real gold somewhere."

Sufi proverb

The Bank of England began issuing bank notes in 1694, printed in black. Soon, the country was over run with counterfeits and they had to buy in special watermarked paper from Sweden that was more difficult to forge. Meanwhile, the Bank of Scotland had to close early in winter, worried that in the poor afternoon light they might mistakenly take coins that had had their edges cut off. It was they who first thought of multi-coloured banknotes printed on both sides.

A banker's life was tough in the days when most British and all US banks printed their own banknotes. With thousands of different varieties in circulation, American shopkeepers needed to keep a big tome called a Universal Counterfeit Detector by the till so they could distinguish the 30,000 different notes in circulation.

In the days of 'wildcat banking' anyone could set up a bank in the American West, print notes, pay for everything they needed – and then simply disappear. Wildcat banking wasn't all bad: it made money available to poor farmers who never would have been lent it by the conventional banks. But it gave the USA two centuries of ruinous bank crashes, like the one in the film *It's a Wonderful Life*. When the United States government started printing the dollar 'greenbacks' in 1862, it was all over for the wildcat banks, but not for forgery.

The biggest attempted forgery in history was a breath-taking piece of Nazi economic warfare, printing £135 million in forged pound notes in concentration camps during World War II, intending to flood the British economy. The plan was impractical so they used the forgeries instead for projects that required heavy payments – like the rescue of Mussolini from an Italian prison in 1943.

Strangely enough, old-fashioned forgery is on the increase – mainly computer-generated counterfeit money, which from $6.1 million in 1997 has been rising steadily ever since. Every year, British bankers confiscate £80,000 in perfectly good notes that appear forged after going through the washing machine; these end up with the other six tonnes of old banknotes that are withdrawn every day in the UK.

But then, what is fake? When the US dollar is backed by such a weight of debt, and by people's continued confidence that it will be repaid, reality may be a problem there too. And these days when bank notes are replaced every few months, and coins are downright inconvenient, the worlds of reality and unreality in money are strangely overlapping. For example:

• About a quarter of a million dollars in new counterfeit money appears daily in the USA.
• One British bank, which accidentally ordered six million 50p pieces, discussed putting them in landfill rather than expensively storing them.
• Parker Brothers have printed more Monopoly money than the US Federal Reserve has issued real money. A stack of all the Monopoly money they have made would be over 1,800 kilometres tall.
• You can buy million-dollar bills on line that look and feel like the real thing, for ten cents.
• $220 million in reproduction dollar bills fluttered off a film set in Las Vegas in 2003 and was spent by passers-by.
• Bank notes were once turned into fertiliser when they were withdrawn. Now they are often made out of polymer plastic, so are eventually melted down and used to make plastic wheelbarrows.

Credit card fraud on the internet (the new forgery) in the USA: $500 million a year

Peter Reuter and Edwin M Truman
Chasing Dirty Money: The fight against money laundering
Institute for International Economics, 2004

Financial markets
The clash of the titans

"Capitalism without financial failure is not capitalism at all, but a sort of socialism for the rich."

James Grant, *Grant's Interest Rate Observer*, 2008

Banks are uniquely profitable businesses, but also uniquely risky ones. Unlike your average corner shop, they take their deposits and lend most of them out again, so at the slightest whiff of rumour or worry about whether they are solvent, all their depositors come running. That is what happens when you get a run on the bank.

The way they deal with the problem is by lending each other money to cover those difficult times when they have less than the amount of cash they need. They lend each other money at a rate of interest called the Libor rate. The 2008 Crash was characterised by an accelerating Libor rate, as the banks began losing faith in each other.

The rage at bankers following the multiple bail-outs in Wall Street and the City of London in 2008 was because they earned vast salaries and huge bonuses, without making much difference to ordinary people and businesses at local level. The truth is worse: the investment bankers' and traders' activities are actively corrosive of the real world where ordinary business makes and does things.

They are corrosive partly because they can be so profitable. Ordinary productive business – certainly when it involves growing things – cannot generate the same level of profit and gets driven out. But they are also corrosive because they give the impression of being the free market at work, when actually it is nothing of the kind.

The sheer insanity of the financial system is enough to make us pretty suspicious, if only because of:

• **Vast fees:** Not just the vast fees charged on handling our pensions – fuelling the insane salaries and bonuses in the financial sector – but the fees earned by brokers who encourage mergers or demutualisations, when research shows most mergers are actually mistakes (see page 63).

• **Pump and dump:** Sending out false rumours over the internet that raise the price of shares, and then profiting when they are sold at the new higher price.

• **Short-selling:** Hedge funds borrow stocks they do not own and sell them, bringing the price down, so that when they buy them back at the lower price they make a profit. This is naked profiting from a company that may have no problem with it – except that it has become a target from hedge fund profiteering.

• **Stupid risk management technology:** Wall Street banks used risk analysis technology to help them reduce the risks in their investments, when actually the programmes are only as good as the data they put in, and that was flawed.

• **Misleading advice:** It seems clear that Wall Street brokers took their clients' money out of safe Treasury securities, which earned the brokers little in the way of commission, and put them into misleading paper savings called 'US Government Fund' which earned them more.

• **Bizarre rewards:** The investors who look after your money are given bonuses for the risks they take, but – if they go wrong – you and the shareholders have to pay the cost.

• **Ridiculous fees:** when bankers pay themselves obscene bonuses, and these have recently been the subject of serious scandal on both sides of the Atlantic. This money comes as a result of the profits from investments – and therefore the money rightly belongs to the bank customers/investors.

The 2008 Crash, and the sub-prime crisis that went before it, revealed that – despite their fees – those who had advised us about money and markets over the past generation were mostly fools, whose narrow outlook had made them blind to risks and realities, whose innocence of megatrends and mega-risks make them unfit to run the world. It is time we rebuilt the financial services sector so that it genuinely supports local enterprise, and returns to the vital but down-to-earth function that we actually need.

The result of this extraordinary combination of lax regulation and fee-based risk-taking is a series of disastrous financial crises:

• **Savings and Loans crisis (1980s):** leading to the bankruptcy of the US building societies.

- **Peso crisis (1994):** the devaluation of the Mexican currency led to capital flight that threatened developing countries.
- **Asian currency crisis (1997–8):** causing disastrous collapses of value in the Far East and Russia.
- **Dot.com collapse (2000–1):** after the internet bubble (see page 131).
- **The 2008 Crash (2007–8)** (see page 133).

Fees earned by the Wall Street brokers organising the merger between Delta and Northwest Airlines (2008): $81 million

Charles Morris
The Trillion Dollar Meltdown
Public Affairs, New York, 2008

Great crashes 1
From Tulipmania to the South Seas

"For an undertaking which shall in due course be revealed."
From a share prospectus during the South Sea Bubble (1720–1)

We imagine that our great financial centres are there to help people invest in shares to raise the capital that business needs to start up, and that there is a little speculation around the fringes as well. That situation has now reversed itself: we raise money occasionally through shares but this is dwarfed by the vast speculative bonanza that takes place on the share markets 24 hours a day across the world.

Occasionally bonanzas cross some invisible line and become quite insane, overturning the status quo and threatening nations with anarchy. Even by the beginning of the 18th century, the author Daniel Defoe was risking arrest by publishing his diatribes against powerful men who pulled the strings behind the speculation.

But by then, the bizarre effects of financial 'bubbles' – when suddenly society goes crazy for dreams of untold wealth and nearly ruins itself in the process – had become clear. 'Tulipmania' in The Netherlands in the 1630s was one of the first bubbles of the modern world. The tulip-jobbers speculated in the rise and fall in the price of tulip bulbs, and many grew suddenly rich when that speculation went out of control.

Writing two centuries later, Charles MacKay, author of *Extraordinary Popular Delusions and the Madness of Crowds*, described how "nobles, citizens, farmers, mechanics, seamen, footmen, maid-servants, even chimney-sweeps and old clotheswomen, dabbled in tulips. People of all grades converted their property into cash, and invested it in flowers. Houses and lands were offered for sale at ruinously low prices, or assigned in payment of bargains made at the tulip-mart. Foreigners became smitten with the same frenzy, and money poured into Holland from all directions. The prices of the necessities of life rose again by degrees: houses and lands, horses and carriages, and luxuries of every sort rose in value with them, and Holland seemed the very anti-chamber of Plutus."

Tulip bulbs that had been bought for people's gardens suddenly reached extraordinary prices, and the rarest were bought for speculation. Strange stories circulated about people who bought them thinking they were onions, ate them by mistake, and found they had consumed the value of a large mansion.

Then the bottom dropped out of the market, the speculators were ruined and aristocrats had to mortgage their estates. Everyone vowed it would never happen again. But it always does – with the same patterns: a belief that some new technological or economic breakthrough has permanently changed the way markets react; doubters are publicly ridiculed, funds for useful projects dry up, and there are assurances that this time it will be different.

Scottish financier John Law persuaded the French government to set up the Banque Royale in 1717, through which he issued large numbers of bank notes that were to be underpinned by profits from his speculative Mississippi Company. There were riots at the Bourse in Paris as people fought, and even sold their bodies, for the right to buy shares. The Banque Royale was soon so successful that Law took on the entire French national debt, turned it into paper and became the richest man in the world.

Fearful that his monster would run out of steam, he employed workmen to march through Paris – ostensibly on their way to South America to dig for gold. But it didn't work. In 1720 the bubble burst and Law escaped, to die later in poverty in Venice. The French aristocracy and middle classes were ruined. The ground had been prepared for the 1789 Revolution.

At the same time the London-based South Sea Company was taking over the British national debt, and speculation in its shares multiplied their value ten times over. Copycat companies joined in the fray with bizarre schemes to develop perpetual motion machines, to trade in hair, to insure horses, or "for carrying on an undertaking of great advantage, which shall be revealed later".

When the chairman and some of the directors of the South Sea Company sold out, the bubble began to deflate, with similar disastrous effects for anyone who had gone from rags to riches as a result. One of the few to sell in time was a small bookseller called Thomas Guy: he was so thankful to escape with his new wealth that he founded Guy's Hospital in London with his money.

In the following century, there was the disastrous speculation in railway shares in the 1840s. Then again, 50 years later, the Bank of England had to save Barings Bank from collapse after its speculation in Argentinian shares. And so on.

Each bubble is followed by an orgy of blame and regulation, which never seems to prevent a recurrence, because of one key omission. "Nobody blamed the credulity and avarice of the people – the degrading lust of gain," said Charles MacKay, writing about the South Sea Bubble at the time of the Railway Bubble. "Or the infatuation which had made the multitude run their heads with such frantic eagerness into the net held out for them by scheming projectors. These things were never mentioned." They never are.

VALUE OF ONE SOUTH SEA COMPANY SHARE 1720

January:	£128
March:	£330
May:	£550
August:	£1,000
September:	£150

Edward Chancellor
Devil Take the Hindmost: A history of financial speculation
Farrar, Straus and Giroux, 1999

Great crashes 2
Wall Street, 1929

"No Congress of the United States ever assembled, on surveying the state of the Union, has met with a more pleasing prospect than that which appears at the present time."
President Calvin Coolidge in 1928. The crash came less than a year later.

Nearly every generation believes its own situation is uniquely safe. Take, for example, the designers of the *Titanic* in 1912 or the designers of the US Federal Reserve system the following year. By the 1920s, it was widely believed that the 'Fed' provided the perfect financial safety net, controlling interest rates and money supply by buying and selling government bonds.

It was the era of Henry Ford's production lines and Frederick Winslow Taylor's implacable time and motion study. The combination of modern factories and new time and motion theories was believed to have created a new 'science' of management. This was a time of rising productivity, docile trade unions, new technologies like radio storming up the stock market, not to mention tax and interest rate cuts; the market seemed unstoppable. No wonder that by 1928 the world's leading economist, Irving Fisher, believed that "stock prices have reached what looks like a permanently high plateau".

An enormous new industry selling stocks was competing to push new ones onto the market even faster. Around 600 new brokerage houses opened on Wall Street in 1928 and 1929; a new investment house opened its doors every day for the first nine months of 1929. "No-one can examine the panorama of business and finance in America during the past half-dozen years without realising that we are living in a new era," said John Moody, founder of the credit ratings agency that bears his name.

Everyone wanted a bit. There were special rooms in some hotels on Broadway where wealthy women could play the market, much to the disapproval of the more traditional brokers. "Everybody ought to be rich", declared the title of a long essay by John Raskob of General Motors in the *Ladies Home Journal* of August 1929, explaining that $10,000 invested in General Motors a decade before was now worth $1.5 million.

You couldn't lose. There wasn't even any need for a financial adviser, said comic actor Groucho Marx, who borrowed a quarter of a million dollars to play the market: "You could close your eyes, stick your finger on the big board and the stock you bought would start rising."

This was dangerous. People borrowed to invest, believing that the market would just keep rising. 'Margin loans' used shares from previous investments as security for the new borrowings; this was to cause a devastating unravelling when the market turned.

The market reached its height in early September 1929, and from October a series of terrifying lurches wiped 83 per cent off the value of American investments. With every lurch, the shares underwriting people's loans lost value too, forcing inexorable rounds of selling and heart-breaking overnight bankruptcies. Groucho Marx, the popular song-writer Irving Berlin and Winston Churchill were among those who lost a fortune – so was Irving Fisher.

"We have involved ourselves in a colossal muddle," said Keynes in 'The Great Slump of 1930', "having blundered in the control of a delicate machine, the working of which we do not understand."

In 1933, the US Congress passed the Glass-Steagall Act to place a strict wall between commercial and investment banking so that a crash never happened again. They busily repealed it again during the dot.com boom of the 1990s. We still don't understand the critical importance of the right kind of regulations.

Value of new securities issued on Wall Street between January and September 1929: $2.5 billion
Proportion which would turn out to be worthless: 50%

John Kenneth Galbraith
The Great Crash 1929
Houghton Mifflin, 1955

Great crashes 3
Junk bonds

"The point is, ladies and gentlemen, that greed, for lack of a better word, is good. Greed is right. Greed works."
> Gordon Gekko, the monstrous trader in the film *Wall Street*, 1987

The explosion of greed in New York, Tokyo and London in the 1980s was partly the result of Margaret Thatcher and Ronald Reagan's deregulation policies. As the party got up steam, it was junk bonds that turned it into a full-scale furnace.

Bonds are simply agreements to pay a specific sum on a specific date in return for a loan. Junk bonds are those that are rated riskier than investment grade; the risk is that the issuer won't pay. The upside is that junk bonds have a higher yield. They allowed companies that couldn't get conventional backing to launch themselves, including the giants MCI and Viacom. The downside is that some of them were extremely risky.

"The securities involve a high degree of risk," said the front page of one junk bond prospectus two days after the 1987 crash, "and accordingly, investors may lose their entire investment."

But that didn't matter. The first new junk bond was issued in 1977 and soon a third of all new bond issues were junk. The revolution came courtesy of the 'Junk Bond King', Michael Milken of Drexel Burnham in Los Angeles, whose new idea launched a wave of hostile takeovers of well-known companies like TWA and RJR Nabisco – dramatised in one of the most successful business books of all time, Bryan Burrough and John Helyar's *Barbarians at the Gate*.

Takeovers like these were known as leveraged buy-outs (LBOs). What the corporate raiders did was to issue junk bonds in the name of the company they were trying to take over, so that the debt fell on the target company once the deal had gone through. Companies that had carefully stayed out of debt became prime targets. Once the raiders had taken them over and sold off the profitable parts, rigorous restructuring was necessary to pay the interest on the great burdens of debt. Tens of thousands of workers lost jobs.

Milken's Drexel Burnham High Yield Bond Conference became known as the 'Predators' Ball' because the most important guests were the corporate raiders who used his junk bonds. Milken got extremely rich, earning a reported $550 million in 1987 alone, but by then the federal prosecutors were investigating. The 1987 crash also wiped about a quarter off the value of companies on Wall Street overnight. He and others were indicted by a federal grand jury in 1989 on 98 counts of racketeering and fraud. A year later, he was sentenced to ten years in prison. He served two years and is now banned for life from financial services, and he spends his time managing a network of charities and think tanks.

JUNK BOND JARGON

Fallen Angels: former investment grade bonds reduced to junk bond status because of the issuing company's poor credit quality.

Rising Stars: bonds with a rating that has been increased because of the issuing company's improving credit quality.

James Grant
The Trouble with Prosperity
Crown Business, 1996

Great crashes 4
The dot.com explosion

"Never before have so many unskilled 24-year-olds made so much money in so little time as we did this decade in New York and London."
Michael Lewis in *Liar's Poker* (1989)

The tech stocks phenomenon of the late 1990s had all the characteristics of a classic bubble: a technological development was supposed to remake the economy completely, nothing would ever be the same again, and the doubters were ridiculed in the press. For a moment, they had many people believing that a website like @Home was suddenly worth the same as Lockheed Martin, or that the internet share-trader E*Trade was worth the same as the giant American Airlines.

The relatively tiny AOL even took over the giant media empire Time Warner – one of the most disastrous mergers of all time. Now most of the dot.coms have disappeared, and even E*Trade decided to open its own bricks and mortar banks.

A handful survived the crash – Amazon, eBay, Lastminute.com and a few others – but the rest were swept away. The whole idea of investors falling over themselves to hand cash to pushy 20-somethings, with their business plans that had no obvious way of making any money back, lasted only a few years.

But once again, those caught up in the bubble believed that this time everything would be different. "We have one general response to the word 'valuation' these days: 'Bull market'," said Morgan Stanley's Mary Meeker, the so-called Queen of the Net. "We believe we have entered a new valuation zone."

Meeker was paid $15 million by Morgan Stanley in 1999 – her top year – for giving advice to investors. The trouble was that the clear divisions that should separate investor advice from the other banking operations in Wall Street had disappeared when the Glass-Steagall Act was repealed. Without those safeguards, tech stock analysts were now supposed to look out for promising companies, sit in on strategy sessions, take new companies public, and – by implication – provide favourable advice that helped sell their shares. Most Wall Street analysts' pay was linked to the banking deals they were involved with and therefore 'advice' was no longer 'detached'.

Meanwhile, the anonymous web bulletin boards hyped pointless dot.com projects and fed the frenzy. By the time sanity emerged, the IT industry had suffered the equivalent of the South Sea Bubble scandal (see page 125) many times over.

Behind the dot.com scandal was the even more peculiar story of the unfolding telecommunications disaster. Thrilled by the prospect of data traffic doubling every three or four months indefinitely, telecom firms around the world put down fibre-optic cable as fast as they could. The work cost $4,000 billion in five years, at least half of it borrowed (the entire output of the US economy is about $10,000 billion per year). The interest on these staggering loans, and the vast sums paid in the UK for third-generation mobile phone licences, crippled the telecoms giants who were forced to sack half a million people worldwide.

Dot.coms, telecoms and the strange world of accounting that hyped the profits of companies like Enron – which claimed to be a dot.com – all made the turn of the century one of the oddest periods on Wall Street.

THE HUBRIS OF TINY DOT.COM START-UPS DURING THE BOOM
Number of dot.com start-ups who bought 30-second TV ads for the 2000 Superbowl: 17
Cost of the ads: $2 million

John Cassidy
Dot.con: The greatest story ever sold
HarperCollins, 2002

Great crashes 5
The 2008 Crash

"We are willing to bet that the agencies assigned too little weight to greed, ignorance, and soft criminality."

James Grant, *Grant's Interest Rate Observer*
on the credit rating agencies, 2008

The credit crunch of 2007–8 and the 2008–9 crash that followed it, are still unravelling around the world, and their full implications may be for the future. By the autumn of 2008, there were barely any independent investment banks left on Wall Street, and no survivals among the demutualised building societies in the UK. President Bush had presided over the biggest bail-out in history and the American model of capitalism seemed as defunct as the Soviet one had been in 1989. Banking will probably recover from the state-subsidised business it has become, because it usually does, but it may be very different.

What led to a global loss of confidence first began as a crisis in the sub-prime mortgage market in the USA, the growing market in mortgages designed for the massive numbers of ordinary families who wanted to own their own homes but could barely afford the repayments – sold as the perfect package.

As such it was a direct result of two things. First, the speculation in homes and 'real estate' on both sides of the Atlantic, forcing house prices to ludicrous levels. Second, the invention of a new way of parcelling up the higher risks of sub-prime mortgages and selling them on to investors around the world. These parcels were called Structured Investment Vehicles (SIVs), and the credit ratings agencies unwisely nodded them through as safe investments.

These bundles of loans included debt from other less risky loans from other markets. This meant that banks and other investors would buy the SIVs, getting the full value of the repayments over the years. The SIVs were then taken apart and reassembled into parcels called Collateralised Debt Obligations (CDOs) and sold to hedge funds, which sold them on all over the world.

Because these CDOs included debts from a range of different markets, they were believed to be insulated against risk. That is how the credit ratings agencies Moodys and Standard & Poor saw it, giving them triple A ratings. The trouble was that, once the truth about the sub-prime loans became clear, this very aspect of the CDOs became their undoing. They could all rely on safe loans being in the package, but they could also rely on unsafe sub-prime loans being in there as well, and – as the default rate on these began to rise – that rendered the whole lot worthless.

When the investigations began in 2007, the banks began calling in investigators like Clayton Holdings in Connecticut. In one mortgage portfolio they checked, they were amazed to find one that had been signed by the borrower as 'M Mouse'.

This was a symbolic moment. If Mickey Mouse could take out a mortgage, then the system clearly had no checks and balances, as you would expect with mortgages sold door-to-door on commission to the poorest, and long after the disappearance of the last local bank manager.

The first losses began appearing that same year when two hedge funds managed by Bear Stearns in New York announced that they had made serious losses by investing in sub-prime loans. They had to sell $4 billion in assets to cover the rush from investors to remove their savings. Nine months later, Bear Stearns was saved from bankruptcy by their timely purchase at a knock-down price by JP Morgan.

By July 2007, Standard & Poor were threatening to cut their ratings on $12 billion of sub-prime debt. A month later, the European Central Bank was pumping 95 billion euros into the money markets, as the interbank lending – which banks need to deal with day-to-day withdrawals while their deposits are out on loan – all but stopped, and the Libor rate which sets the cost of money lent between banks, began to shoot up. A month after that, reports that Northern Rock was looking for emergency financial support from the Bank of England led to the first run on a British bank for over a century, with the alien sight of investors queuing for hours in the rain outside branches.

Those who suffered most were the people who had taken out sub-prime mortgages in the USA, one in five of the total. Two million foreclosure proceedings began in the USA in 2007 alone, many against people sold mortgages where the terms and interest rates were misrepresented to them.

By the end of 2007, mortgage lending was a fraction of what it had been, loans were difficult to find, and banks had written off about half of the estimated $1 trillion of losses around the world. Meanwhile, the price of oil rocketed as speculators looked for other assets to invest in, in the short term.

By the end of 2008, it was clear that the crisis was much more serious. The collapse of the Lehman Brothers in New York led to a stock market plunge and goverments around the world, but especially in London and New York, were forced to step in and save their struggling banking sector from collapse. As this book goes to press it is clear that the crisis is far from over.

EARNINGS FOR ONE CREDIT RATING AGENCY ON WALL STREET
2000 $159 million
2006 $705 million

Larry Elliott and Dan Atkinson
The Gods That Failed: How Blind Faith in Markets Has Cost Us Our Future
Bodley Head, 2008

Future crashes
The derivatives market

"Weapons of financial mass destruction."

Businessman and philanthropist Warren Buffett's
description of derivatives, *Fortune*, 3 March 2003

Welcome to the modern world of arcane financial instruments, and
perhaps even to the world of the next Great Crash. Derivatives are
fiendishly complex, and they cover anything that isn't tangible: the right
to buy raw materials at a future date at a set price, or the underwriting
of a risk that someone won't be paid by someone else. Derivatives are
not about the rate of growth but the rate that growth is growing, and the
rate that 'second' growth is growing too.

It's all about offsetting risk – because it is all about buying options
on shares rather than the shares themselves – and that can be useful
for companies who need to protect against future risks. But when
derivatives become the subject of speculation, and the deals go wrong,
they can multiply losses many times over, and that can be disastrous too.

The first hint of trouble in the early 1990s hit the German company
Metallgesellschaft, followed in quick succession by nine-figure losses by
Cargill, Procter & Gamble, Daiwa Bank of Japan and Orange County,
California – before trader Nick Leeson's bet on a rising Japanese stock
market in 1995 destroyed the 225-year-old Barings Bank.

Then there was Long Term Capital Management (LTCM), run by two
American academics. The idea was to hedge and protect their bets, using
$3 billion they had been lent to buy derivatives with a notional value of
$1,250 billion. But the Russian debt crisis of 1998 upset their complex
mathematical predictions and they were soon losing $500 million a day.
The US Federal Reserve was afraid for the world's banking system and
bailed them out with $3.6 billion.

But the risk is vague because the experts on derivatives hide away in
the secretive hedge funds – using derivatives to make money as markets
slide. They reveal nothing, not even who works for them. Hedge funds
tend to be registered in offshore financial centres (see page 54), and they

market themselves just to the very rich. Managers tend to take one per cent of the invested funds and 20 per cent of the profits in their pay packet, so the results have to be spectacular.

These days the most famous hedge fund managers, George Soros, Julian Robertson and Barton Biggs, have made way for a new generation of even more shadowy and unregulated successors.

Some of them are also immensely ambitious. Soros made $2 billion when he led the run on the pound on Black Wednesday in 1992, when it dropped out of the European Monetary System. It also seems likely that there was a tacit conspiracy among hedge funds, during the financial crisis of 1998, to target the Australian dollar. In fact some hedge fund managers warned the Australian treasury that resistance was futile.

But was the conspiracy bigger than that? Some economists believe the whole crisis of 1997–8 – with hospital patients across the Far East thrown out of their beds and on to the street because their currencies had collapsed – was the result of a hedge fund conspiracy that went out of control.

Ten years on, the foolhardy banks had realised that derivatives were a way that corporations could create money outside the usual banking liquidity rules. Derivatives are not quite money – they are contracts to buy things at different times and prices – but they can be used as money. By 2007 the value of derivatives in the market had increased to a terrifying £516 trillion – the entire GDP of the world is only $50 trillion.

Worse still, very few people – and not even the greatest living investor Warren Buffett, or the chairman of the Federal Reserve – quite understand how they work.

Value of derivatives market (2008):   £500 trillion
Value of global output (2008):   about £30 trillion

Peter Temple
Hedge Funds: The courtesans of capital
John Wiley & Sons, 2001

Calming the money flows
The Tobin Tax

"The collapse of the global marketplace would be a traumatic event with unimaginable consequences. Yet I find it easier to imagine than the continuation of the present regime."

George Soros, *Soros on Soros*, 1995

The financial establishment believes that the sloshing of vast sums of money across the wires of the money system – $3,000 billion a day, remember, most of it speculation – makes the economic system efficient. The traders react quickly to efficient governments by buying their currency, and act just as quickly to punish inefficient ones.

George Soros and his Quantum Fund were, between them, the most famous hedge fund double act in the world during the 1990s – until he withdrew from active management after mis-timing his reaction to the dot.com boom and losing a packet. Soros was one of the first insiders to warn the world of the perils of the system's inbuilt instability: traders earn more when the market veers wildly than they do when it is stable.

Nor are the dangerous interconnections in the global marketplace the only risk, or the computers that are programmed to sell automatically when the market drops a certain amount. The whole theory behind the markets is flawed, said Soros: it doesn't tend towards equilibrium at all, but overshoots and veers off dangerously in the wrong direction.

In the 1997 crisis, where currency after currency across the Far East collapsed in the markets – with devastating consequences for the people who lived there – people began to ask whether there were alternatives, or at least some speed bumps to slow down the flow of capital. Even the famously laissez-faire UK Prime Minister Tony Blair began talking about the consequences of an 'absence of discipline' in the markets. Here are some possible solutions to the instability:

• **The Malaysia solution:** Malaysian prime minister Mohamed Mahathir re-established exchange controls in 1998, preventing people from taking large sums of money out of the country – the situation all over the world until 1979. As a result the Malaysian recovery was faster than its neighbours'.

• **The Columbia solution:** lets foreigners invest in local businesses but not buy debt or shares, which means they can't simply sell up overnight.

• **The Chile solution:** Any foreigners investing in the country have to keep their money there for a year – which deters speculators.

• **The Tobin solution:** This was the brainwave of Nobel Prize-winning economist James Tobin in 1971, who suggested a small 'levy' on foreign exchange transactions of 0.05 per cent. This would be enough to calm down the speculation, but it would also raise enough money to put the UN's Sustainable Development Programme into effect. This is now known as the 'Tobin Tax'.

The Tobin Tax is very controversial – Tobin himself changed his mind about it – but has been backed at various times by the Canadian and the French governments. It would fail if one of the main financial centres remained aloof, and they would all have to agree. But if governments were allowed to keep half the money they collected from it, that could be a sufficient reward to get them moving.

Recent years have seen a number of variant proposals aimed at paying for the UN Millennium Development Goals, set at lower than Tobin's original proposal, and designed so that individual countries can go it alone. So far they are not doing so.

THE SIZE OF THE PROBLEM
World financial flows every day (1996): $1.5 trillion
World financial flows every day (2007): $3 trillion
World central bank reserves (2007): $4.5 trillion

www.ceedweb.org/iirp

Let the poor pay tax
The strange world of tax avoidance

"Only little people pay taxes."

> Leona Helmsley, disgraced New York property owner,
> attributed to her by her housekeeper in 1989

Income tax is a radical idea in itself. It means that people pay to keep the social fabric together, amongst other less useful things, according to what they can afford. That is the main reason why the tax, first introduced in Britain to pay for the Napoleonic Wars, has been such an icon of the political Left.

The problem is that, thanks to a whole range of changes in the past quarter century, paying income tax has become compulsory for ordinary people but increasingly voluntary for those able to afford expensive accountants and tax avoidance advice (see page 63).

But the growth of tax havens, and competition between national tax authorities – and the new world of instantaneous financial exchanges – has had an absolutely massive impact on corporation tax, because companies can avoid paying tax by registering in tax havens. The result is that small companies pay their taxes, but their global competitors generally don't.

Two thirds of international corporations in the USA paid no tax at all between 1996 and 2000. As many as 90 per cent of the rest paid less than five per cent of their earnings. In Europe, the picture is less extreme, but pretty similar.

Governments connive at this extraordinary loss because they have, perhaps without admitting it even to themselves, lost confidence in open markets and competition. They prefer a few powerful whales to a cacophony of competing minnows. They like the idea of giant corporations, with the muscle to do their bidding and the monopolistic power to control inflation, and are prepared to subsidise them to keep them sweet (see page 80).

What can be done to make sure that corporations pay their fair share, and compete fairly with the minnows?

- Clamp down on the tax havens (see page 54).
- Regulate capital flows (see page 138).
- Insist on transparency anywhere in the world where companies are based, and an end to secret bank accounts.
- Shift to green taxes, on pollution or carbon, which are harder to avoid (see page 76).

There is evidence that some tax authorities are beginning to clamp down on tax havens. Germany is breathing down the necks of the secretive banks in Lichtenstein. US authorities are insisting on the right to trace money that might be used by terrorists. Yet still the biggest companies are failing to pay their fair share.

**Estimate of the tax gap in the USA in 2007
(the amount of tax owed but not paid): $345 billion**

www.taxjustice.net

The new multi-billionaires
The world of Bill Gates

"Money is like muck, not good except it be spread."

Francis Bacon, *Essays*, 1625

One peculiarity of the speculative 'success' of recent years is how little wealth has 'trickled down' to the poor. The economist Paul Krugman estimated that up to 70 per cent of the extraordinary US economic growth of the 1980s was delivered to the richest one per cent of the population. There were 13 billionaires in the USA in 1982, and by 2005 there were 341.

Similar disparities exist between the people of the world as a whole. The poorest 20 per cent of countries now have less than one per cent of world trade, a quarter of what they had a generation ago.

The vast wealth has partly been driven by ridiculous pay packages for chief executives, often no matter how unsuccessful they are. Disney's CEO Michael Eisner first made executive pay a political issue when he was paid a package worth $575 million in 1998 – about 25,070 times the average Disney worker's pay, and far more than that if you count the low wages paid in factories in Honduras or Bangladesh that make Disney shirts and bags.

Of all the wealthy individuals, the most outrageously so has been Microsoft founder Bill Gates. When Windows 2000 was launched, Gates's personal stock of Microsoft shares rose in value by more than $130 billion – or 12 times more than the entire securities owned by the whole population of African-Americans.

Yet the most successful managers were also being rewarded for their role in driving down the wages of those at the bottom end – increasingly employing immigrants who are ignorant of their rights, which is why, even in the USA, the average wage has been sinking slowly since the beginning of the 1960s.

The question is whether democracy can survive with gigantic disparities in wealth and power, or whether, as the economist Jeff Gates puts it, the system is 'making the world safe for plutocracy'. For example:

• Three billion of the world's population live on less than $2 a day.

• The world's 200 biggest corporations account for as much as 28 per cent of world economic activity but employ less than 0.25 per cent of the global workforce.

• The world's 200 wealthiest people own the same amount of wealth as the combined annual income of the poorest 2.5 billion people.

• A fighter aircraft sold to a poor country costs the same as education for three million children in the developing world.

• African-Americans owned half of one per cent of the net worth of the USA in 1865, the year slavery was abolished. By 1990 this had crawled up to one per cent.

Does anyone in the world really deserve to earn more than £1 million? Executives are now credited with extra years to their pensions as a way of getting round criticisms about pay – often while they are busily cutting employees' pension rights (see page 95). Yet when Carly Fiorina was forced out as CEO of Hewlett Packard in 2005 because she failed to deliver target profits, she still took away a bonus of $42 billion. Her replacement got a golden hello of $20 billion, plus his annual salary which amounted to a similar figure every year. Richard Grasso was ousted as head of the New York Stock Exchange in 2003 after it emerged he had accrued $190 million in deferred compensation.

**Annual remuneration of Yahoo chief
Terry Semel (2005): $109 million
Time it would take someone on the US
minimum wage to earn that: 11,000 years**

Jeff Gates
Democracy at Risk: Rescuing Main Street from Wall Street
Perseus, 2000

Section VI

Local money

When international money flows become a super-highway, speeding vast sums across the world, then local economies that are in any way peripheral tend to lose out. But that is not the end of the story. Local economies are learning how to claw some of it back.

Money flows
What goes around comes around

"Money is round, and it rolls away."

Confucius, 5th century BC

Whether money works for your neighbourhood is not just a matter of how much of it there is locally. It isn't about counting up everybody's wealth, or working out how much money a new development will bring in. There are so many poor places that still have rich people and valuable projects at their heart. The important question is not "How much money comes in?" but "Where does it go to afterwards?"

Does it come in and stay, circulating around the local businesses, adding to the wealth every time it does so? Or does it seep straight out again the way it came, to tax bills, utility bills, outside professionals or supermarkets? Take two communities, for example:

• One has a supermarket, which pays some of its takings to local employees, then banks the rest to be invested in the money markets. Studies of very dependent communities, like Native American reservations in the USA, have found that three quarters of their money leaves again within 48 hours – to pay bills to distant utility companies, or to shop in Walmart, which every night sends all its takings to Arkansas.
• The other community has a range of small shops, and when any of the shopkeepers need something, they can buy it locally. What is earned by one shop is used in the next and so on. Not only is the town centre vibrant and alive, but the small businesses are in charge of their own destiny. Owners have resisted being transformed into reluctant supermarket employees.

Both communities have the same amount of money coming in, but one is an economic desert and the other is thriving, sustainable and 'real'.

Money that stays circulating locally is like lifeblood: it keeps communities alive. It brings together the people who need things done with the people who have the time and raw materials to do them. Otherwise local life just grinds to a halt and dies.

The way that even a small amount of money can add to local wealth just by circulating around is known as the Multiplier Effect. It was first described by two disciples of Keynes, Joan Robinson and Richard Kahn, and applied to nations. Slowly governments and local authorities are beginning to apply the same idea to cities and communities.

A study by the New Economics Foundation in Cornwall in 2000 found that a pound spent on the local vegetable box scheme circulated in the local economy nearly twice as far as a pound spent in the local supermarket. The same year, Knowlsey Council in Merseyside measured their local multiplier effect and found their local economy had become a seriously leaky bucket – only eight per cent of their expenditure even reached local people. All the rest was siphoned off by consultants, big corporations and outside contractors.

Northumberland County Council discovered that they could increase the impact of their regeneration spending four times over just by looking at where the council was buying their food for school meals, or their contractors for parks, and all the rest of their procurement. Now all the councils in North East England are rolling out a programme called LM3 (Local Money 3) – it measures three circulations of any money spent in the local economy, which in turn measures the impact of different spending options. They can, for example:

• Train up local small businesses and voluntary sector workers to bid for their contracts.
• Make sure contracts are divided up into manageable lots which small bidders can manage.
• Develop the local food and agriculture sector.
• Set up business training that genuinely links people into local networks, like BizFizz, the business coaching model pioneered by the New Economics Foundation and the Civic Trust.
• Make sure there is genuine competition for local procurement – there are now only two giant waste contractors left in the UK because of monopolistic procurement practices.

The sad fact is that most modern investment is more like an umbrella than a funnel. The trickle-down effect – the idea that money spent on the rich will eventually trickle down to the poor – simply doesn't happen. At best the poor receive just that small trickle.

We invest vast sums in regeneration schemes that rarely result in genuine regeneration for the people who live there. Architects design the places, and big regeneration companies swing by, but the result is somewhere that is dependent on outside capital and looks the same as everywhere else. A range of diverse local businesses are more likely to stay put, more likely to spread the wealth around, and more likely to create a sense of local well-being, than a couple of large retailers run by a board of 'fat-cat' directors in London or New York.

Amount spent at a supermarket to create one local job: £250,000
Amount spent at a corner shop to create one local job: £50,000

Justin Sacks
The Money Trail: Measuring your impact on the local economy using LM3
New Economics Foundation, 2002

Local diversity
The basis for life

*"Variety's the very spice of life
That gives it all its flavour."*

William Cowper, *The Timepiece,* 1785

Wander through an ancient English woodland, whether in Yorkshire or Sussex, and you will find a cornucopia of different plants, animals and insects. You will find streams and fields next door that have names that go back maybe a thousand years.

Increasingly, scientists believe that it is the sheer complexity of these biological and eco-systems that gives them life and keeps them healthy. Money can do the same to economic systems when they work well, providing the glue which allows people with things that need doing to link up with those who want to do them.

But when money goes wrong, either because it measures values badly (see page 64) or because it demands too great a return (see page 83), then it can drive out that diversity. Then you get woodlands that all look the same, with line upon line of quick-growing and regimented conifers. Or you get single cash crops that drive out the diversity of the small market gardens. Or bland identikit high streets, or worse still, dead ones.

The trouble is that economists in developing countries often overlook diversity, because they only count the production of the one staple crop they are interested in. The figures go back to their development agency, and all the rest that was grown is forgotten – pushed out in the pursuit of huge monoculture acreage driven by foreign aid and development.

Genetically modified (GM) seeds are the application of this kind of mistake to the business of farming. These single varieties of seed are designed to stop farmers using their traditional methods of saving seeds for the following year. They infect other varieties and the monopolistic seeds drive the others out, leaving farmers at the mercy of the agribusiness giant that owns the rights to the seeds.

That is the tragic policy that has led to the suicides of farmers in India, and elsewhere. In fact, developing countries often remain productive without GM, where people are still growing in the traditional way – despite the rhetoric by the apologists of the GM industry that theirs is the only way to feed the world:

• In Java, small farmers cultivate 607 species in their home gardens.
• In sub-Saharan Africa, women cultivate as many as 120 different plants in the spaces left alongside the cash crops, and this is the main source of household food security.
• A single home garden in Thailand has more than 230 species, and African home gardens have more than 60 species of tree.
• A study in eastern Nigeria found that home gardens occupying only two per cent of a household's farmland accounted for half the farm's total output.
• Home gardens in Indonesia are estimated to provide more than 20 per cent of household income and 40 per cent of domestic food supplies.
• UN research has shown that small biodiverse farms can produce thousands of times more food than large, industrial monocultures.

Global corporations find this hard to understand, says the scientist Vandana Shiva: "Global consultants fail to see the 99 per cent of food processing done by women at household level [in India], or by small cottage industry, because it is not controlled by global agribusiness; 99 per cent of India's agro-processing has been intentionally kept at the household level. Now, under the pressure of globalisation, things are changing. Pseudo hygiene laws that shut down the food economy based on small-scale local processing under community control are part of the arsenal used by global agribusiness for establishing market monopolies through force and coercion, not competition."

Suicides of farmers in India in 2003:   17,107

Vandana Shiva
Earth Democracy: Justice, sustainability and peace
South End Press, 2005

Local life 1
The attack of the monster ghosts

"There was no there there."
Gertrude Stein on Oakland, California, *Everybody's Autobiography*, 1937

Take a walk along a British high street, especially in the south-east. If you are of a forgetful nature, you could quite easily forget which town you are in: they all have the same ubiquitous shiny shopping centre, the same shops, the same brand names, the same brands. And a terrible parallel blight seems to have afflicted small towns: the whole diversity that used to make these places throb a generation ago has gone.

Where have the local shops, post offices, pubs, butchers, police stations, doctors and railway stations gone? We are no poorer – quite the reverse – so where did all those playing fields go? Or the local postal deliveries and local newspapers? The conventional explanations do not wholly explain why it is so hard to afford the simplest public services, health, post and education when we are so wealthy.

What seems to happen, according to a 2001 report by the New Economics Foundation, is that small towns and villages reach a 'tipping point'. There is no slow, smooth curve of economic decline, but a sudden collapse.

Each closure is bad enough on its own: in the UK, a quarter of all bank branches and fishmongers disappeared in the 1990s, and the 222,000 grocery shops that existed in 1950 have come down to 35,000 today. But when the number of local retailers falls below a critical mass, the quantity of money circulating within the local economy suddenly plummets, as people find there is no point trying to do a full shop in town.

Even if only half the population does a small amount of shopping at a new superstore, this can be enough to bankrupt the town centre, because very little supermarket revenue stays circulating in the local economy. Then you get a rash of abandoned buildings and fly-posting. Many rural communities are now dangerously close to their tipping point, thanks to the slow decline of local banks, local pubs and more recently local post offices.

A century ago, every town had its own newspaper packed with local news and local advertisements. Now very few places can support them. Other losses include:

- six wholesalers close every week
- 2,000 small shops closed in 2006 alone
- 1,500 football pitches have been lost in London since 1989
- one third of the UK bank branch network closed from 1992 to 2002
- 60 cottage hospitals closed in 2002 alone
- the average person travels 893 miles a year to buy food
- only 18 per cent of public parks are in good condition.

What has been causing this catastrophic throttling of local life? Is it too much television or too much targeting of public spending in the inner cities? Is it the monopolistic supermarkets or out-of-town shopping centres? The answer is: it is all of these things and more.

But there is some good news. If small towns and villages can hold off their own tipping points a little longer, the years of declining local life may be over. One of the clear causes of ghost towns is low oil prices and, as those prices get more expensive – and it becomes more difficult to centralise food distribution or drive to the shops, or send consignments of biscuits to Italy for packaging – then we can expect a re-localising of all these services and a demand for something better.

But will government ever re-localise its police, health service and justice services?

Lowest price of a barrel of oil (2003): $25
Highest price of a barrel of oil (2008): $140

www.localworks.org

Local life 2
The attack of the monster clones

"Developers are like urban Domestos. They destroy 99 per cent of all known distinctiveness."

Hugh Pearman, *Sunday Times*, 2004

The medieval Northgate in the city walls of Oxford, where Archbishop Cranmer was held before his execution, was finally knocked down in 1904 to make way for traffic. A mere seven decades later they banned traffic from the Cornmarket anyway, but the gate was gone for good.

The massive impact of traffic and shopping centre development has had a devastating effect on the distinctiveness of our town centres and high streets. Wander down the high street of cities like Reading or Swindon and you could be in any high street from one end of the nation to the other.

Driven by high rents and monopolistic retailers, we all suffer from 'clone town Britain', a phrase coined by the New Economics Foundation. Instead of real local shops, we have developed towns which include a near-identical package of chain stores. As a result, the individual character of many of our town centres is evaporating. Retail spaces once filled with independent butchers, newsagents, tobacconists, pubs, book shops, greengrocers and family-owned general stores are becoming filled with supermarket retailers, fast-food chains and global fashion outlets.

Many town centres have lost their high streets' distinctive facades, as local building materials have been replaced by identical glass, steel and concrete storefronts that provide the ideal degree of sterility to house a string of big, clone-town retailers. It is a phenomenon that affects people whether they are rich or poor, as the *London Evening Standard* recognises in its continuing Save Our Small Shops campaign.

In times of recession, the first stores to close are often the clones, just as Woolworths led the way in the recession that began in 2008.

Does it matter if local history is bulldozed and replaced with an information board, or bland national brands replace distinctive local names and styles? Yes it does, because:

- **Economics:** People want to live and invest in places that have a history and are distinctive. Evidence suggests that property prices and rents rise by five per cent if there are small distinctive shops nearby.
- **Money flows:** Chain stores tend to siphon earnings out of the local economy as well as driving out smaller local competitors, which makes local economies more vulnerable to economic downturns.
- **Social capital:** Local stores look out for local crime, advise local people and provide a meeting point. They inoculate high streets against disorder and are a critical part of the social glue.
- **Democracy:** Research in the USA by two economists (one from Pennsylvania State University, the other from the American University in UAE) showed that people living near a Walmart store tend to vote less.

What can we do about it? The Office of Fair Trading suggests that once any one company gets more than ten per cent of the market there will be market distortions, including rising prices, damage to suppliers, loss of diversity and choice. So we probably need monopoly-busting legislation that forces market share, nationally and locally, below that ten per cent. We need new local markets, which even now provide food cheaper than the big high street names. We need local forums and 'retail trusts' to limit sudden rent rises that can devastate local businesses, in favour of sustainable rises in value that benefit everyone. We also need investment in small business and local enterprise, backed by the procurement power of local government.

And we need people to be aware that they need to use locally owned stores or they may lose them. But the evidence is that this message is beginning to get through.

Proportion of souvenirs sold in London tourist shops that are made in London: less than 5%

www.commonground.org.uk

Local competition
Unravelling the cosy subsidised world of the big corporates

"Vigorous in youth, rapidly turning complacent in middle age, before either becoming senile or an arm of the industry they are meant to regulate."
John Kenneth Galbraith on regulators, *The Great Crash 1929*, 1955

Go to the small Oxfordshire market town of Bicester and you won't find a great deal of choice about where to shop. In a town of just 30,000 people there are no fewer than six Tesco stores. One of the peculiarities of modern money is that it is presided over by a host of regulators to make sure that there are no 'market irregularities', who in practice have presided over a massive growth of monopoly.

The whole logic of modern business is that rival businesses must combine in order to compete with other vast combines on another continent. So Tesco is allowed to build up a one third share of the UK grocery market and Waterstones is allowed one third of the books market because it has to compete with Tesco, and so on.

The number of pharmaceutical companies has shrunk to a handful of global monsters. The local banks of the UK, which once underpinned local enterprise, have disappeared completely in a half-century of lucrative mergers (see page 156). Worse, the giants salt away their earnings offshore, and make use of government regeneration subsidies and tax breaks, none of which are open to their smaller competitors.

This means that the Big Four supermarkets have enough monopoly power to force suppliers to accept payment in 90 days, providing themselves with a rolling interest-free loan big enough to demolish any smaller competitor. Only suppliers with nowhere else to go could possibly agree to such terms, especially as they also have to pay hefty introduction fees to the Big Four for stocking their products at all.

In practice, governments have given up on free, open markets because they find it more convenient to deal with a handful of powerful behemoths. The result is the kind of combination of corporate power allied with state power that Hilaire Belloc warned about in 1912, in his book *The Servile State* (see page 158). This tyrannical combination of capitalism and socialism uses the rhetoric of free trade but actually turns its back on competition. It contains the seeds of a new kind of oppression: the subjugation of everything to corporate efficiency and government-sponsored profitability. When the Bush administration funnelled a giant $10 billion monopoly contract to one company for reconstruction in Iraq it underscored their belief that somehow monopoly meant efficiency.

This is the kind of capitalism where spin is substance. When seed manufacturers say their GM seeds do not drift, then – when they grow uninvited on neighbouring organic farms in Canada – the farmers are prosecuted for theft.

A handful of international companies have built up unprecedented control over key industries, especially agriculture:

• The top 30 food-retailing corporations account for one third of global grocery sales.
• One large transnational corporation controls 80% of Peru's milk production.
• Five companies control 90% of the world grain trade.
• Just six companies control three quarters of the global pesticides market.

Power Hungry: Six reasons to regulate global food corporations
ActionAid, London, 2005

Local banking
The key to local enterprise

"The loss of the last bank caused more damage to village trade than the arrival of an out-of-town Sainsbury's."
Richard Smith, butcher in King's Langley, Hertfordshire, 2001

In the 1970s television comedy *Dad's Army*, the bank manager is the central figure. Self-important, pompous and mildly Churchillian, Captain Mainwaring represented generations of British high street bank managers. They were frighteningly respectable, careful and risk averse, but they provided local banking services to the local economy.

A series of mergers swept the local banks away, and they have been replaced by another Big Four (HSBC, Barclays, Lloyds and RBS) that range in their enthusiasm for their high street banking network from dull acceptance to downright contempt, as they buy up and close down our remaining building societies as well.

HSBC, which devoured the Midland Bank, had the nerve to call itself the World's Local Bank, and to take an equally global giant Interbrew to court for the right to do so. But you are no longer able to phone its local branches – you are put through to international call centres which operate using formulas to decide what you are allowed to do, and which may or may not have your particular problem on their screen.

At the same time there was a flurry of takeovers, especially during the years 1999–2001, which saw Royal Bank of Scotland (RBS) take over NatWest, Bank of Scotland take over Halifax, Barclays take over Woolwich, and the Spanish bank Santander take over Abbey National, leading to a whole range of closed branches and shuttered shops. More recently taxpayer support and partial nationalisation have propped up many of those which have survived.

The disappearance of local banks, along with the disappearance of local post offices, has had a disastrous effect on small businesses. They have to drive further, and queue much longer, to bank their takings or deal with money. Other nations have managed to keep a competitive local bank network, and there are new alternatives emerging:

- **Agricultural banks:** In Europe there is still a thriving network of agricultural banks and landesbanks, originally set up to lend to farmers but also lending to other small and regional businesses.
- **Credit unions**: These are still small scale in the UK, but most towns in the US have at least one sizeable high street credit union which has kept the local bank network intact.
- **Community Development Finance:** Like the South Shore Bank in Chicago or the London Rebuilding Society in the UK, these funnel loans into voluntary housing, social enterprises and other projects which the giant banks find hard to handle (see page 107).
- **Local community banking partnerships**: like the Robert Owen Community Banking Partnership in Welshpool, providing a combination of credit union, debt advice and other services (see page 107).
- **Community banks:** which provide shared services to the other banks, and keep local branches running.
- **Post office banks**: like BancoPosta in Italy, which provides an economic underpinning to the postal network and postal services to customers that the big banks avoid, providing them with e-cash cards. They are now the biggest issuer of electronic debit cards in Europe.

It is all a long way from the days before 1862 when every American bank was able to issue its own money, a risky situation which some campaigners in the United States remember with affection. But at least local banks have human beings to run them, rather than computers. The rule of the local bank managers was inconvenient, but they knew where their loans and mortgages were going. Their demise contributed to the the credit crunch of 2007–9, which saw billions of dollars lent to home owners who could not afford the repayments (see page 133).

Percentage of UK bank branches closed since 1990:   40%

www.communitybanking.org.uk

Local solutions 1
Distributism

"Do anything, however small. Save one out of a hundred shops. Save one croft out of a hundred crofts. Keep one door open out of a hundred doors; for so long as one door is open, we are not in prison."

GK Chesterton, *The Outline of Sanity*, 1926

Nearly 80 years ago, a group of inexperienced political campaigners – outraged at the monopolistic behaviour of the London General Bus Company – took the unprecedented step of launching their own pirate bus service. They leased a series of ancient omnibuses, painted them in rainbow colours and called them 'Morris', 'Ruskin' and names with similar radical echoes, and took on the giant bus company on its most lucrative routes.

The campaign failed. London General swept all before it, including the small bus operators the campaigners were defending, only of course to be nationalised under the auspices of the London Passenger Transport Board in 1933.

The campaigners' views on this nationalisation are unrecorded, but they would not have approved. The 'Distributists', as they called themselves, believed that giant state-run enterprise was indistinguishable from giant corporate enterprise. The problem was one of size and ultimate power.

Distributism dates back primarily to Hillaire Belloc's 1912 book *The Servile State*, written just after the end of his period as a Liberal MP. In it he set out the basic premise: that free market corporatism and socialism both end in much the same place: centralisation and a kind of slavery. He and GK Chesterton argued for solutions based on small-scale ownership – the very opposite of Fabian socialism at the time – as the only guarantee of freedom against the corporate giants.

If you owned your home, a vegetable patch, maybe a small business, you could never be impoverished, dependent or forced to do anything against your will in quite the way that you could if you were simply at the beck and call of Big Manager or Big Bureaucrat. Distributism meant:

- small-scale land ownership, allotments and similar
- massive anti-trust legislation to break corporations down to a manageable size
- giving away homes and land to those without them
- a massive revival of crafts and self-help.

Distributism became increasingly sidelined by a Roman Catholic approach to economics, which was influenced by Pope Leo XIII's 1894 encyclical that introduced the term 'subsidiarity'. This is the idea that government is at its most humane when it is conducted at the lowest possible level.

Despite a number of innovative projects in the 1930s and '40s, encouraging unemployed people to grow their own food, by the 1950s Distributism had all but died out and is now almost forgotten as a political creed. Belloc and Chesterton are both dusty figures from a bygone age, their greatest works unread and their reputations – like those of many political figures of the 1920s and '30s, right and left – a little tarnished by a note of anti-Semitism (although in their defence, they were among the first to warn of Hitler's true intentions).

But there are some signs of a revival of interest, especially now that corporate power and the size of institutions are back at the forefront of the wider political agenda – thanks primarily to the writer Naomi Klein.

Number of allotments in the UK in the wartime Dig for Victory years: 1.4 million

Amount of food produced in allotments and back gardens per year in the war years: 1.3 million tonnes

Number of allotments in 2008: 300,000

GK Chesterton
The Outline of Sanity
London, 1926

Local solutions 2
Consumer co-ops

"Political reform from the kitchen"
The Seikatsu Club's political slogan (1980s)

History remembers the late 1960s as the years of student revolt. In Tokyo, they also marked a fascinating revolt by women in one district, led by Fusushi Yokiko, who was frustrated that local shops were failing to stock healthy food for themselves and their families. In response, they formed the Seikatsu Club, which grew into probably the biggest and most successful food co-operative in the world.

Their campaign to persuade local shops to stock the food they wanted turned into a co-op which pooled resources to pay for better quality milk to be brought into the city in bulk. But that was just the beginning. Within a decade or so there were 100,000 members across Tokyo, organised at street level, where families paid for their own healthy food and the co-op produced it, through their own bakery and a series of farms.

Soon they were also employing members in their own homes, making sandwiches and preparing other food. By the 1980s they were getting their members elected to local government bodies under the slogan 'political reform from the kitchen'. There are over 150 Seikatsu members elected to public bodies, out of over 200,000 members.

The Seikatsu Club is now a significant business enterprise, with annual retail sales around £500m. They have started over 400 workers' collectives running restaurants, bakeries, used goods stores, soap factories and caring for elderly people. They employ 15,000 people.

Consumer co-ops can make a difference by pooling resources and multiplying market power. The Japanese community-supported agriculture schemes have now spread to the USA, via the followers of Rudolf Steiner in Europe, allowing people to buy into harvests for individual farmers.

This provides farmers with the income when they need it, and provides members with healthy local food throughout the year.

These schemes are a potent antidote to big agri-business. The biggest one is Farm Fresh to You, with 4,000 members, in California.

Co-operatives are an effective way of pooling know-how or buying power which can make local economies work, and they don't have to be consumer co-ops. Other examples include:

• **Mondragon:** in the Basque region of Spain, where the local Catholic priest inspired a series of linked workers' co-ops to employ local people when he arrived in 1941. There are now over 150 co-ops, and taken together they are the seventh biggest corporation in Spain.

• **SEWA:** the Self-Employed Women's Association, an organisation of 40,000 women textile workers all over India which band together to cut out the middlemen and sell their textiles direct.

• **John Lewis Partnership:** a worker's co-op, and now one of the most successful retail companies in the UK.

NUMBER OF COMMUNITY-SUPPORTED FARMING VENTURES IN THE USA:
1990: 60
2008: approaching 3000

www.rodaleinstitute.org

Local solutions 3
Transition Towns

"I've found that climate change deals with the invisible and has very little positivity about it, whereas this is all about positivity. Everybody can get stuck in and design the change – it is very much a bottom-up initiative."
Duncan Law, *Transition Town Brixton*, 2008

Rob Hopkins trained in permaculture design and was in the process of building his own straw-bale house in southern Ireland when it was deliberately burned down in 2004. He had also been involved in a project called the Kinsale Energy Descent Plan, which was to re-imagine the town where he lived in a world that was using considerably less fossil fuels.

The loss of the house precipitated a shift from Ireland to Devon to study the idea of 'energy descent plans' more broadly. If the moment of 'peak oil' – the theoretical high point of oil production, after which energy prices rocket – is upon us, then what in practice can communities do for themselves to re-organise their economies and lives to survive?

The question led to the Transition Towns movement, which hit the zeitgeist in its response to climate change in 2006, initially in Totnes where Rob had gone to live. It is a 12-step programme to re-engineer and re-skill the local community, drawing in some ideas from the Local Agenda 21 movement of the 1990s, but with more ambition. New kinds of energy, new currencies (see page 167), new kinds of distribution and new kinds of decision-making structure, are all emerging from the towns and villages that have designated themselves Transition Towns.

Following the success of Transition Town Totnes, there are now well over 100 Transition Towns declared around the world, making the first tentative steps. As far as money is concerned, those steps include finding ways of keeping it circulating locally and maximising the amount of local production, linking to renewable energy, sometimes as a way of paying for some of the other projects – as well as growing their own vegetables, baking their own bread and mending their own clothes.

This practical activity is part of what the movement calls the 'great re-skilling', which means that – to make the transition – we are going to have to re-discover those skills that were often second nature to our forebears: bread-making, sewing, food cultivation and health.

The Totnes pound (see page 185), launched by Transition Town Totnes in 2007, received major news coverage. When it came to the launch of the Lewes pound in East Sussex in 2008, nearly every national news outlet dashed to the town to cover it. Even the BBC radio soap opera *The Archers* has been considering whether to make Ambridge a Transition Town.

THE TRANSITION TOWN 12-STEP PROGRAMME

1. **Set up a steering group and design its demise from the outset**
2. **Raise awareness**
3. **Lay the foundations**
4. **Organise a Great Unleashing**
5. **Form sub-groups**
6. **Use open space**
7. **Develop visible practical manifestations of the project**
8. **Facilitate the Great Re-skilling**
9. **Build a bridge to local government**
10. **Honour the elders**
11. **Let it go where it wants to go ...**
12. **Create an Energy Descent Plan**

Rob Hopkins
The Transition Town Handbook: from oil dependency to local resilience
Green Books, Totnes, 2008

Local solutions 4
Local Alchemy

"I mean, where did all the money go?"
Glen Jenkins, Marsh Farm, Luton, 2008

Taken together, ideas like local money flows and small business coaching
(see pages 145–6) amount to an important critique of the regeneration
industry, and the powerful voluntary sector agencies that cluster around
it applying for government grants and contracts – a process known to
more cynical academics as 'farming the poor'.

Agencies dedicated to tackling poverty come to need poverty to
continue in order to carry on getting the grants they need to keep their
staff employed. They need the poor as much as the poor need them, just
as they need the Lottery, which has become in some ways a recycling of
"hard-earned pennies" into middle-class charity workers.

The problem is that decades of massive investment in regeneration
has had little or no impact on poverty. There are shiny new buildings,
maybe Olympic facilities, but the same old social problems remain,
because regeneration agencies have not seen it as their business to
develop the skills and know-how of local people, or to see where the
money ploughed into regeneration goes afterwards.

Local Alchemy is a package of sustainable regeneration ideas,
developed between the New Economics Foundation and the East
Midlands Development Agency, which sees people's assets as broader
than simply the money they haven't got. Those assets include the money
that flows through their area, their relationships, imagination and skills,
and the vital confidence to work with others. Bring all those together
and you have real regeneration that works for local people and for the
planet as well.

When the Marsh Farm estate in Luton worked out that they were
spending a collective £1 million a year just buying fast food from outside
the estate, they set up a community business to provide healthy fast food
to keep the money circulating locally. Then they rented some unused
local fields to provide some of the potatoes and vegetables.

Sustainable regeneration is a process which recognises these assets and helps local people to challenge the status quo, building towards:

• a diverse range of businesses and enterprises in terms of size, social and private mix, and diversity of goods and services produced
• positive local money and resource flows (a high local multiplier and local re-use of waste)
• a strong local asset base, including local people's attitudes, skills and knowledge, physical, financial and natural resources
• a responsive public and business sector that works to strengthen and invest in the local economy
• a strong community and civic voice, including local activism, leadership, volunteering, and engagement in debate
• sustainability and a reduced environmental footprint
• an increased understanding of the economic, cultural and ecological interconnections that link communities, span the globe and impact on the future.

Value to the local economy of spending £10 in a Cornish branch of a supermarket chain: £14
Value to the local economy of spending £10 in a nearby vegetable box scheme: £25

www.pluggingtheleaks.org

DIY money

What do neighbourhoods and towns do when they are sidelined by the global money superhighway? Well, for a start, they can try creating their own …

Creating money
The challenge of doing it yourself

"Singapore and Hong Kong, which are oddities today, have their own currencies and so they possess this built-in advantage. They have no need of tariffs or export subsidies. Their currencies serve those functions when needed, but only as long as needed. Detroit, on the other hand, has no such advantage. When its export work first began to decline it got no feedback, so Detroit merely declined, uncorrected."

Jane Jacobs, discussing the advantages of city currencies,
Cities and the Wealth of Nations, 1984

Banks create money, governments create cash, businesses create shares. So why can't we all create the money we need?

This is not something we can do entirely by ourselves, although pop star David Bowie issued Bowie Bonds back in 1997 as a way of drawing forward some of his predicted future income. But when communities, neighbourhoods, towns or cities run short of cash – because it has all flowed somewhere more lucrative – then it can make sense for them to start to issue their own.

National currencies, like the pound and the dollar, tend to be geared to the financial services sector. They are information systems that respond to what the City of London and Wall Street feel are important, but they don't work nearly so well in manufacturing areas or in poorer suburbs, for example.

Yet those marginalised places may have everything they need for success – people who want to work, people who need jobs done, raw materials that can be put to use – but lack the cash they need to bring them all together. The banks refuse to create it for them, and the investment money may prefer to shoot down the wires to the City to frolic among the hedge funds or whatever scheme is in vogue at the time. Creating their own money may be the imaginative leap they need.

Creating your own cash has a long and honourable tradition. Only in the 12th and 13th centuries did kings first try to get control of all the money, and a terrible hash they have made of it ever since. In the USA it was not until the end of the Civil War that the government took the exclusive power to issue cash themselves – though of course banks can do the same using a signature on a cheque or a computer keystroke. Since then, all the following have been used as money when the 'real' stuff has got scarce:

• **Beads and precious stones:** Early settlers in North America bought Manhattan Island from the native Americans for $24 worth of beads.

• **Tea**: The Chinese used square packs of tea as currency for thousands of years. The Chinese word for these was 'cash'.

• **Tobacco:** especially in wartime, when cigarettes became universal currency – particularly the bad ones (the good ones were smoked).

• **Paper:** Benjamin Franklin's efforts at the printing press were one of the many causes of the American War of Independence (see page 39).

• **Air miles:** The US company Northwest Airlines paid their entire public relations budget in air miles throughout the 1990s.

• **Tokens:** The Global Barter Clubs of Argentina had over a million members using tokens as currency, allowing people to barter surplus stock, vegetables and other mutual support.

• **Out-of-date stock:** Companies increasingly use business barter exchanges to trade things like out-of-date stock, or hotel rooms on specific dates that are too imminent to sell in the normal way. Up to a fifth of world trade is now carried out using electronic barter currencies like trade dollars (see page 176).

If they can do it, why should impoverished towns and communities wait helplessly around for the government to rescue them – when they know perfectly well they won't – and when they have all the bare necessities they need locally? They can issue their own money and start using their own assets more efficiently.

That is what different kinds of money do: they are information systems that measure the value of local assets differently from the big currencies. Big currencies don't recognise local young people, old people, dilapidated buildings, or parks as assets. They don't realise that all the computers, white goods and furniture we throw away in perfect working order are actually assets. If we can design currencies that value them better, then these assets will be used. These will not be national currencies, but 'complementary'.

That is the challenge for the DIY currency experts, and it is one they meet in a variety of ways. They know their new currencies need to be backed by something – whether this is the trust of the people who use them, local produce (see page 174), locally produced renewable energy or other commodities – otherwise nobody will use them. They also know they need to be available enough to be useful, otherwise only the rich will get them. Every DIY currency mixes these functions – free money (medium of exchange) and real money (store of value) – in different ways. That is the point about money: it has to be real but it also has to be readily available.

Yet most modern money achieves neither of these. It is fiat money, created out of nothing by banks and worth something because the government says it is (see page 40). We need new kinds of money, invested in new ways, to put local people and small business first.

You will never get rich inventing your own money – although some of the dot.com internet currencies like beenz and i-points did briefly turn their creators into multi-millionaires on paper during the dot.com boom (see page 131). But local money could get the exhausted wheels of the local economy turning again, and it could provide new values that the current money system conspicuously lacks.

Number of complementary currency experiments in the world: about 5,000–9,000

Thomas Greco
Money: Understanding and creating alternatives to legal tender
Chelsea Green, 2001

Money that rusts
Irving Fisher and Stamp Scrip

"The purpose of Free-Money is to break the unfair privilege enjoyed by money. This unfair privilege is solely due to the fact that the traditional form of money has one immense advantage over all other goods, namely that it is indestructible."

Silvio Gesell, the Argentinian trader who came up
with the idea of rusting money, 1913

It is always going to be easier to make money out of money, rather than using it to do something productive, said the Argentinian trader Silvio Gesell in 1913, because money grows if you invest it – unlike real commodities that tend to rust or go mouldy if you hang on to them. The answer, he said, is to have money that rusts too. That would mean that the interest rate would be negative: it would cost you money to hold on to your money.

His idea was taken up enthusiastically during the Great Depression, most dramatically in the Austrian ski-ing town of Wörgl. And by catching the eye of the great US economist Irving Fisher, rusting money was adopted all over the world before it was declared illegal.

As a result, only one of the great 1930s money experiments is still running: the Wirtschaftsring system in Switzerland, a mutual-credit currency scheme widely used by the building industry and the restaurant sector. Wir, as it is called, started in 1934, the brainchild of Werner Zimmerman and Paul Enz, two of Gesell's followers. By 1993 it had a turnover of £12 billion, using a parallel currency to the Swiss franc. They renounced Gesell's 'negative interest rate' in 1952 and now pay and charge low interest on loans and deposits.

Wörgl was in a terrible state during the Great Depression when the burgomaster Michael Unterguggenberger persuaded the town to issue its own currency, to the value of 30,000 Austrian schillings, known as 'tickets for services rendered'. But unlike ordinary money, these notes lost value by one per cent a month, and to keep their value – if you hadn't spent them – you had to buy their stamps once a month and stick them on the back. The proceeds of the stamps went on poor relief.

The notes circulated incredibly fast. Within 24 hours of being issued, most of them had not only come back, via shops and businesses, to the municipality in the form of tax payments – months in advance – but had already been passed on again. During the first month, the money made the complete circle no fewer than 20 times. After four months, the town had built public works of 100,000 schillings, employed the jobless and paid off most of the town's tax arrears.

Fisher was inspired by what he found in Austria and rushed out his own instruction manuals, called '*Stamp Scrip*', for the struggling American towns. Within months, about 300 US communities were printing their own negative-interest money.

But on 4 March 1933 it was all over. President Roosevelt, advised that the monetary system was in danger, banned Scrip systems and gave the existing ones a short time to wind themselves up. As he did so, he created the conditions for a final flurry of activity. Fearing a complete collapse of the American banking system, he closed all the banks – and all over the country, communities and companies had to provide some kind of alternative to money. "I care not what kind – silver, copper, brass, gold or paper," said one senator from Oklahoma. One community in Tenino in Washington State even produced its own wooden money.

As the Stamp Scrips were shut down on one side of the Atlantic, the Austrian National Bank was taking action to suppress the Wörgl experiment too. Four years later, Austria was annexed by Nazi Germany.

Stamp Scrip might not provide the stability people need for real money – money they can use for savings – but it might as well serve for exchange money.

NUMBER OF CORPORATE MEMBERS OF THE SWISS WIR SYSTEM:
1934:   16
2005:   62,000

Richard Douthwaite
*Short Circuit: Strengthening local economies
for security in an unstable world*
Lilliput Press, 1996

Real money
Keeping it constant

"For in every country of the world, I believe, the avarice and injustice of princes and sovereign states abusing the confidence of their subjects, have by degrees diminished the real quality of the metal, which had been originally contained in their coins."

Adam Smith, *The Wealth of Nations*, 1776

People usually become interested in creating their own money in times of economic hardship. When that hardship stems from a clampdown on the amount of money in the economy, then people look for ways of creating currencies that are more available. But when the hardship is spiralling inflation, they look for something that is more reliable. One of the most fascinating experiments in creating money was for an inflation-busting currency in the 1970s. It was the brainchild of Ralph Borsodi, then in his eighties, and one of the founders of the green movement. He warned of coming inflation a good quarter-century before it became a problem – the only bestseller he ever wrote was called *Inflation is Coming* (published in 1945) – and he predicted the post-war flight of population from the cities on both sides of the Atlantic. He also worked with Irving Fisher during the Depression to help him develop his '*Stamp Scrip*' (see page 170).

Enraged by growing inflation around the world, which he regarded as a government fraud on the public, Borsodi became fascinated with the possibility of inventing a new kind of money that would keep its value because it was based on something real. Over lunch in Escondido, California in 1972, he picked up a copy of the *New York Times* and found that the Federal Reserve was devaluing the dollar. In fury, he sat down and designed what he called an 'honest money system'.

Later that year, he launched the 'constant' currency in his home town of Exeter, New Hampshire. What was revolutionary about the 'constant' was that its value was tied to a basket of commodities. It was also backed by $100,000 of his own money, on deposit in banks in Exeter, Boston and London.

Borsodi's main problems were: how to choose these commodities, how to buy them as backing, and how to store them. You could hardly put $100,000 worth of oil and wheat in your garage, let alone in the bank. So he arbitraged them instead, organising a team of supporters to buy shiploads of the chosen commodities while they were at sea in tankers and sell them straight on – and meanwhile make a profit.

By February 1973, the University of New Hampshire Press was printing 275,000 'constants' in different denominations up to 100. Exeter's local council even started accepting them as payment for parking fines. His economist friends at the university were working out how to keep the value steady, while young volunteers dealt with paperwork and the media. Bemused locals tried to understand why their constants were worth $2 one week, and $2.05 a week or so later.

Having proved that a constant value was possible and that people would use it, Borsodi wound the experiment up. It has never been repeated. His main disappointment was that it failed to enrage the Federal Reserve. But officials were relaxed about it: "They can circulate clamshells or pine cones if they want to," they told the press. "As long as people accept them."

UK INFLATION AFFECTING CHEDDAR CHEESE
Cost of 1kg of cheddar cheese (1930):   17p
Cost of 1kg of cheddar cheese (2008):   £9.00

David Boyle
Funny Money: In search of alternative cash
HarperCollins, 1999

Money as vegetables
Printing your own

"I guess the only solution is to print your own money."
Frank Tortoriello, Deli Diner, Great Barrington, Massachusetts, 1991

Frank Tortoriello was the proprietor of a small café in the Massachusetts town of Great Barrington, when his bank turned down his request for a $5,000 loan so that he could move to bigger premises. When he asked the EF Schumacher Society based nearby for advice, they suggested that he issue his own money.

The result was deli dollars, a series of notes designed by a local artist and marked "redeemable for meals up to a value of ten dollars". The café would not be able to redeem all the notes at once after the move, so Frank staggered the repayments over a year by putting a date on each note after which it would be valid. To avoid counterfeiting, he signed every note, one by one like a cheque, and he sold them for $8 each. He raised $5,000 in a month.

The notes were an enormous success. Contractors bought sets of deli dollars as Christmas presents for their construction crews, parents of students at the nearby college knew they would be a good present for their children. Even the bankers who turned down the original loan request supported Frank by buying them. The notes turned up in the collection plate of one local church because the congregation knew the minister ate breakfast at Frank's café. Frank repaid the loan not in dollars, but in sandwiches.

The idea was the brainchild of the great American social innovator Bob Swann, a carpenter who spent two years in prison as a conscientious objector during World War II, much of it in solitary confinement because he refused to accept the prison's racial segregation rules. During that time, he came under the influence of an associate of Gandhi's and found himself thinking deeply about money. The deli dollar idea was his and it spread under his influence.

Two local farms took up the idea of issuing 'greensbacks' to recover from a fire and to help them pay for heating their greenhouses through the winter. Customers bought notes in the autumn and cashed them in for plants and vegetables in the spring and summer. The result was the Farm Preserve note. They were designed with a head of cabbage in the middle surrounded by a variety of other vegetables. The notes carried the slogan 'In Farms We Trust' and were sold for $9 each.

The Farm Preserve notes, like the Monterey general store notes and Kintaro notes that followed, gave local residents a way to support the kind of small independent businesses that help to make a local economy more self-reliant. They have all now been superseded by the much more ambitious and successful Berkshares currency, which covers Great Barrington and the surrounding area (see page 184).

Swann was concerned about underpinning the value of the money – but also of making it more available by basing its value on local products, like locally produced energy, or chickens, or firewood. We have these assets locally, he said, and they can be used to raise money. We are not as poor or dependent as we think.

ASSETS YOU COULD BASE THE VALUE OF A LOCAL CURRENCY ON:
Firewood (New England)
Chickens (Kentucky)
Local renewable energy (Sweden)
Beef (Argentina)
Potatoes (Ireland)
Tulips (Holland)
Corn (Caribbean)
Cheese (Wisconsin)
Wave energy (Scotland)
Books (Hay-on-Wye)

www.schumachersociety.org

The rise and rise of barter
Swap shops

"Money is too important to leave to central bankers."
Milton Friedman, quoted in *Chicago Sun-Times*, 2001

In traditional societies, barter kept the wheels of the economy turning without cash. If you grew carrots, you could swap them for whatever else you really needed. But economists are wary of barter, and despair when an economy collapses so badly – as in the former Soviet Union in the 1990s – that highly complex barter deals re-emerge, like carrots for tyres, for radio batteries, for cabbages, for neckties and so on.

Barter is certainly highly inefficient, because you need to have what the other person wants. But barter using the new kinds of electronic currency is very efficient, and is currently on the rise all over the world. Economists barely recognise it, official statisticians ignore it and so it is a phenomenon that is barely studied. But we know that:

• **It is big:** It now covers somewhere between 10 and 20 per cent of world trade, and much more if you include the old-fashioned barter deals – known as countertrade – that are direct swaps. One of the most famous countertrade deals was responsible for first putting Russian vodka into Western shops.

• **It can get you out of a hole:** Barter is what economists call 'counter-cyclical'. When the economy slides into recession barter goes up, and vice versa. Not much economic activity works like that.

• **It measures things better:** Barter can give value to your stock even if the global currencies think it is valueless. If you were unwise enough to stock up on purple toothpaste, for example, or if you have hotel rooms on specific dates or airline seats that are about to expire, or you want to clear your office of last year's computers – and five million perfectly good computers are put into landfill in the UK every year – then using barter currencies can give these items value.

Three big barter exchanges dominate the world of barter: Active International, ICON International and Atwood Richards, and their clients include two out of three of the Fortune 500 companies, the annual list of the biggest companies in the world. But local barter for small business is also growing rapidly. Nearly all business barter companies, known as 'exchanges', issue their own electronic money called trade dollars or trade pounds as a way of facilitating transactions, which – because it can be insured in the USA – is increasingly taking on some of the attributes of hard currency. There are now over 2,000 business barter exchanges in the USA, involving about 845,000 businesses.

Barter is also becoming increasingly sophisticated. When your local exchange can't immediately find what they need for a deal, they can use an international currency called 'universal' to barter it from elsewhere. But the key point is this: if the biggest companies in the world – and some of the smallest – can all use DIY currencies, and benefit from them, why can't the rest of us? Economists say that these ideas are irrational and primitive, yet most of the most successful companies in the world are doing it.

Total value of barter trades in the USA (2006): $30 billion
Proportion of Fortune 500 companies bartering: 60%

Terry L Neal and Gary K Eisler
Barter and the Future of Money
Master Media, 1996

DIY money 1
LETS

"On the morning after the Depression a man came to work building a house, and the foreman said to him, 'Sorry chum you can't work today. There ain't no inches.' He said 'What do you mean there ain't no inches? We got lumber, we got metal, we even got tape measures.' The foreman said, 'The trouble with you is you don't understand business. There are no inches. We have been using too many of them and there are not enough to go around.'"

Alan Watts, *From time to eternity*, 1960

One of the paradoxes of money is that it has become little more than blips of information (see page 51) – just a measuring system that we pretend is also valuable. But that does lead to some peculiarities. To say there isn't enough money is like saying there aren't enough inches, said Michael Linton, originator of LETS, making use of Alan Watts's example.

Nor is this just a metaphor. It is insane to use a measuring system for a medium of exchange like money, only to find that the measuring scale is missing. You may have someone to do a job for you, the raw material for the job and the demand for it, but no money to bring all those things together. In France in 1848, the radical Pierre-Joseph Proudhon launched a People's Bank which – although it was swept away by that year of revolutions – allowed the money to be created automatically in that kind of situation. The buyer would simply create a debt, denominate it – not in pounds or euros – but in some agreed currency, and pay it off later by doing work themselves. That was the idea behind the explosion in local currencies in the 1980s, starting with David Weston's Community Exchange in Vancouver and Michael Linton's Local Exchange and Trading System (LETS) in Canada's Comox Valley.

Weston was a social innovator and academic; Linton was an Alexander Technique teacher. LETS rapidly spread across the English-speaking world in the 1980s and the French-speaking world in the 1990s, but it began as a mutual-credit money system, called 'green dollars'. People and businesses decide the rate and conditions for accepting the community currency instead of normal cash, which they negotiate with customers. You may need cash for the tax and the cost of materials from outside the local economy, but you can use other kinds of money for other aspects of the purchase. So you issue your own money in green dollars, and by doing so, you are 'committed' to honour it, redeem your money, and keep your promise.

The transactions are tracked, normally using a computer programme. In the UK, where LETS spread to almost 400 schemes during the 1990s, a series of bizarre and colourful names were used for these – 'bricks' in Brixton or 'bobbins' in Manchester.

Linton's first LETS began in 1983. Within two years it had turned over the equivalent of $300,000 in 'green dollars' trading, including vegetables, room rents and dentistry. What is exciting about LETS is its simplicity. It did not attract the attention of regulators and officials who might have been concerned that this was some kind of 'bank'. There was also no problem about how much should be issued. The debits and credits on the system always exactly equalled each other: when you buy with LETS, you create a credit that can be spent by somebody else.

LETS is normally taxable, like barter trade dollars, but governments have generally been confused about how to treat LETS for welfare purposes. New Zealand and The Netherlands are among those to have passed laws encouraging unemployed people to use local currencies. UK cities like Liverpool and Sheffield experimented with LETS as a way of building community spirit on poverty-stricken housing estates, but there is never much motivation for money experiments during boom years.

Yet local currencies like LETS are on the rise around the world, especially in Japan and the Far East. The South African Community Exchange System is increasingly successful, and the first LETS are emerging in Hungary, Indonesia, Nigeria and Ecuador.

Transition Towns developing a local currency (2009): about 150

Peter North
Money and Liberation
University of Minnesota Press, 2007

DIY money 2
Community way

"Any community, network, business, can create its own free money – 'free' as in free speech, free radical, freely available, but not free as in 'free lunch'."
Michael Linton and Ernie Yacub, *Open Money Manifesto*, 2000

Imagine a world where everyone had not only an email address, but also a community currency address, which they could use to create money in as many different currencies as they might want – a village currency, a babysitting currency, a city or regional currency, or an international currency for plumbers, for example. The currencies could suit different aspects of their lives.

The system already exists on the internet and it is breathtakingly simple, set up by the man who began LETS (see page 178), Michael Linton, who has spent the last two decades working out how to make a money system that can simply provide people with what they need without them having to get a bank loan.

Embedded within it is a whole new idea about how communities can provide themselves with the money they need; it is sponsored by business but costs them nothing. Known as 'community way', it has been tested out by communities on the Canadian west coast. The idea goes like this:

• Local businesses create the electronic local money in the form of donations to local charities (at no cash cost to them because this is local money, though they do have to pay for the electronic equipment).
• The charities sell these to local donors in return for pounds or dollars.
• These people then use the local money to buy what they want – all the participating businesses agree to accept it on their own terms, maybe 20, 50 or even 80 per cent of the normal price – whatever makes sure that their basic cash costs and taxes are covered in national money. The local money carries on circulating until it returns to the original business that issued it, which is then encouraged to spend or donate it on again, keeping the loop going.

It sounds like a trick, but is far from being that. Businesses accept local money to attract new customers, and it saves them money from their marketing budget. Everybody wins, because local businesses are playing the same role as banks – creating money out of nothing. And the local money keeps the lifeblood of the local community working.

'Community way' is an imaginative response to the way some local communities are running out of cash, and it is has already worked in:

- **Rural Ireland:** The 'Roma' currency (Roscommon Mayo) was run as an EU-funded experiment. Roma notes were issued into the local economy by the local radio station. They then circulated and were eventually accepted back in return for advertising.
- **Minneapolis:** The Commonweal project developed a dual-track credit card, with dollars and time credits earned helping out in the community. They were accepted as part payment for goods and services in the biggest shopping mall in the USA, outside Minneapolis.

The point of Commonweal, said inventor Joel Hodroff, was that the mainstream economy was infinitely productive. That meant you could take points like babysitting credits and give them buying power in the main economy. Restaurants that struggled to cover costs on Sundays could attract new diners by accepting part payment in credits, while covering their costs in dollars.

Taken together, these ideas and community way provide the basis for a whole new multi-currency world, using different credit systems to underpin different aspects of our lives (see page 193).

TESTBEDS FOR 'COMMUNITY WAY'
Comox Valley, British Columbia
Santa Cruz, California

www.openmoney.org

DIY money 3
Hours

"Hours is money with a boundary around it, so it stays in our community. It doesn't come to town, shake a few hands and then wander out across the globe. It reinforces trading locally."

Paul Glover, founder of Ithaca hours, 1999

The kind of DIY money you design depends on what specific problem you are trying to solve. One of the key problems with modern money for towns like Ithaca in upstate New York is that money that comes into the town tends not to stay.

A generation ago, money earned in a community would stay there circulating like lifeblood (see page 145), and every time it was spent in the small shops it would carry on going round, bringing wealth and cashflow with every exchange. These days, all too often, it flows straight out again – to big utilities or big retailers. Small towns shrivel up, and the planet is heated up further by trucking vegetables across continents.

In Ithaca, the community activist Paul Glover, became interested in money when he was working on a radical plan to improve the flow of energy around Los Angeles. He dreamed up the Ithaca hours currency after listening to the story of deli dollars (see page 174) on the radio.

His 'Ithaca hours' currency works like this. There are printed notes in denominations of 1 hour, 2 hour, half hour, quarter hour and eighth hour (each hour is worth $10) which are issued into the economy every month in three ways:

• In payment to people who advertise in *Ithaca Money*, the bi-monthly tabloid newspaper which lists the main businesses and services accepting hours – in return for public backing and for keeping entries up to date.
• In grants to local charities and non-profit groups: 9.5 per cent of every month's issue is decided by the 'Barter Potluck' – a meeting of anybody interested on the 15th of every month.
• In interest-free loans to local people and businesses. The biggest local currency loan in the world – equivalent to over $30,000 – was recently made in Ithaca hours to help the local credit union build new premises.

Ithaca hours were launched in 1991, with the parody slogan on them 'In Ithaca we Trust', and were an immediate success. They are now accepted at over 300 businesses in the town, backed by the mayor and chamber of commerce and accepted at some of the town's banks.

Glover believed that, because the local currency could only be spent within a 20-mile radius of Ithaca, it could stem the flood of buying power out of local economies. Ithaca's surviving town centre and massive thriving farmers' market seem to prove he was right. Hours have been shown to give a marketing advantage to local businesses that accept them, to provide more income for people on the margins of the economy, to substitute local products and services for those flooding in from outside – and to make the local economy more sustainable, diverse and able to survive recession or inflation.

Glover personally keeps in touch with as many of the hours users as possible, making sure the currency does not gather anywhere in the system – and if it does, sorting out where it could be spent. It is not easy to launch your own currency and work out how much should be in circulation at any one time without creating the equivalent of inflation.

More than 80 other towns across North America have tried the same thing with varying degrees of success. Some have thrived because of the collectable quality of the notes, like the Salt Spring Dollars in British Columbia. But the initiative for this kind of printed currency shifted in the late 1990s to Latin America, where the Global Barter Clubs of Argentina – currencies using printed notes – were for a brief period keeping up to two million people alive.

Value of hours in circulation in Ithaca at any one time: about $100,000
Limit of interest-free loans in hours available to small local businesses: $5,000

www.ithacahours.org

DIY money 4
Discount notes

"Using Berkshares will be a citizen's way of voting for local businesses and keeping money local."

Susan Witt, EF Schumacher Society, 2006

Ithaca hours were designed to keep money circulating in the local economy (see page 182). The new wave of discount notes on both sides of the Atlantic are designed more precisely to help local shops to fight off competition from out-of-town shopping malls and the identikit 'clone town' corporate chains that leach money out of local high streets.

They have learned many of the lessons of the local currencies that blazed the trail, and are based on the experience of the pioneering EF Schumacher Society in Great Barrington, Massachusetts. Their deli dollars, farm notes and Berkshares experiments led the way to the launch in 2006 of their new Berkshares currency, named after the Berkshires region of Massachusetts.

Berkshares are discount notes. You buy the equivalent value of $10 for $9 in one of the local participating banks (and New England has the enormous benefit of still having a thriving and innovative local banking system, whereas local banks in the UK have long since been snapped up by four corporate behemoths). You can change them back into conventional dollars any time, minus the discount, which means people can afford to take risks with the currency. The big chains do not accept Berkshares so they re-circulate locally, encouraging local business and local activity, and encouraging people to buy local and use local resources where possible.

There is the equivalent of $2 million in circulation in the Berkshires region. It practice the system gives people a discount of ten per cent at any locally owned business in Great Barrington, a major built-in benefit for small stores in the high street, which continues to thrive despite its flyblown destruction in so many other US towns. Similar ideas are built into local loyalty cards in the UK like Wedge, which gives cardholders discounts in participating local stores without a circulating currency. The success of Berkshares has led a number of the Transition Towns (see page 162) to start planning similar currencies themselves. The Totnes pound launched in 2007 and is already accepted by 70 local businesses. But the launch of the Lewes pound in Sussex managed two important firsts for complementary currencies in the UK – wall-to-wall press coverage and the enthusiastic participation of the local branch of Barclays Bank. More Transition Towns are currently planning their own, so watch this space.

Number of local bank branches around Great Barrington that accept Berkshares: 11

www.berkshares.org

DIY money 5
Time banks and time dollars

"Market economics values what is scarce – not the real work of society, which is caring, loving, being a citizen, a neighbour and a human being. That work will, I hope, never be so scarce that the market value goes high, so we have to find a way of rewarding contributions to it."
Edgar Cahn on the thinking behind time dollars, 1999

The pioneering law professor Edgar Cahn was concerned about the money system because it only values what is marketable. That can sometimes make it toxic for communities and families, and all those vital human skills that we rely on – to socialise young people, look after the elderly and unwell, be 'good neighbours' and keep the streets safe – get forgotten and disappear (see page 64).

But he has a solution, which he calls 'co-production', which sets up a series of reciprocal relationships between professionals, public services and agencies and their clients, using a tax-exempt electronic currency called 'time dollars' or 'time credits', operated through 'time banks'. People earn time by helping out in their neighbourhood, and they spend time when they need help themselves from other neighbours – not professional help like healthcare, but the sort of mutual support that everybody needs occasionally.

Cahn hit on the idea during a prolonged stay in hospital after a heart attack in 1980, where he found himself hating the sense of uselessness that he felt there. He persuaded a healthcare foundation to launch six experimental schemes in the USA in 1987. There are now over 100 time banks in the UK, with many more in Japan, China, the USA, Spain and other countries.

The result is a parallel currency, more a medium of exchange than store of value, that focuses on making neighbourhoods work better – reconnecting people, giving value to people outside the market, and restoring trust. Time banking recognises that almost everybody has something that the community needs, even if it is simply providing a friendly voice over the phone.

Professionals like doctors, teachers or police can't succeed without the active involvement of the community, said Cahn, and time banks provide a way of redefining work so that it includes all this vital but unmarketable work – looking after older people, checking on people coming out of hospital, measuring and rewarding this effort. This is seriously radical money.

Time banks are a solution for our struggling welfare bureaucracies, with increasingly exhausted professionals dealing with increasingly disempowered clients, who are never asked for anything back. They provide a way that both sides can work together so that welfare, health services, education and all the rest actually work. They mean that clients can 'earn' credits also for extra training, such as sports coaching or computer training. They create a reciprocal relationship that turns welfare beneficiaries into equal partners who are earning by doing the work that society needs.

Cahn believes that only a massive and unprecedented increase in volunteering, and using the human skills that exist in such abundance in every community behind closed doors, can tackle the enormous social problems we face, ranging from crime to ill-health. There will never be enough money to pay professionals to do all this work, and professionals are not good at providing mutual support networks for people anyway. But the work will have to be rewarded somehow, and time banking provides a way of doing this.

Time banks give back responsibility to people who are regarded as 'the problem' or useless. By so doing, they transform their lives. Teenage jurors in Washington now cash in their time dollars in return for refurbished computers. Prisoners in Washington earn them by keeping in touch with their children. People with depression earn them by looking after older people. Some innovative projects include:

- **Cities:** Networks of time banks are now emerging across cities like London and St Louis, connecting up projects in a range of different ways so that they support each other (St Louis has linked this into the health system so you can pay doctor's bills in time).
- **Schools:** Struggling schools in Chicago and Albany pioneered the idea of paying time credits to pupils as peer tutors, which they cash in for refurbished computers. Academic results go up and bullying goes down.

• **After-school clubs:** Children in the Slovak city Zilina have organised their own network of six time banks, and contribute to ambitious activities in their after-school club.

• **Housing:** Residents in one public housing complex in Baltimore have been paying part of their rent in time.

• **The law**: People in Maryland and California can pay for legal advice in time; some have paid this off by taking part in demonstrations outside the offices of bad employers.

• **Prisons:** Women ex-prisoners in San Diego pay for aftercare services in time, paid off by providing support to each other. The UK government is pioneering time banks in prisons.

• **Health:** Health centres and health insurance companies are paying time credits to patients for supporting neighbours and even – in Catford – doing basic DIY. Research in Brooklyn shows that people earning time tend to stay healthier.

It costs money to set up time banks – they need a co-ordinator – but the rewards are potentially huge. This resource can plug dwindling budgets and the holes in our pensions. One group of hospitals in Richmond, Virginia, cut the cost of treating asthma patients by more than 70 per cent in two years, by paying them in time to befriend other asthmatics. Similar ideas lie behind the Fureai Kippu currencies in Japan, where people help in their community for the price of a home-cooked meal, and similar schemes.

Time banking reconnects people, builds networks and rebuilds trust. They may also be very important in the future, as policy-makers search desperately for ways to revitalise neighbourhoods.

Number of time credits earned in UK time banks: 602,500

Edgar Cahn
No More Throw-away People: The co-production imperative
Essential Books, 2000

Green money
Currencies that make us sustainable

"The notion of multiple target currencies opens up a new way of thinking in economics."

Edward de Bono, *The IBM Dollar*, 1994

Airline accountants flew into a panic some years ago when they realised that their clients had issued three trillion frequent flyer miles over the previous ten years that were still unspent. If they were all to be spent at once, it would bankrupt the airlines. If any of their executives doubted whether Air Miles or Nectar Points were a kind of money, the airline accountants were quick to explain that they were.

The discovery led to a massive re-think about Air Miles and other reward points. Companies are now much more cautious about what they issue and most make sure their points expire if you don't use them. Tesco has issued 25 million Clubcards, which allow shoppers to collect points. But more worryingly, they also allow issuers to snoop into cardholders' shopping baskets and personal tastes.

But loyalty points can be more subtle than ordinary money. They are an information system that can use spare capacity to get people to behave in a certain way, and that is just as relevant to cities as it is to companies. Witness the extraordinary success of the Brazilian city of Curitiba, which issued points to people for recycling their rubbish. They were enthusiastically collected by street children handing in litter off the streets. The points could be spent on the buses during off-peak times. As a result Curitiba is the cleanest city in Latin America, and it's all paid for by spare public transport capacity.

Rotterdam experimented with an even more ambitious project, backed by Rabobank and the transport and waste departments of the city council. Nu-SpaarPas paid electronic points on to a personal smartcard to reward green behaviour – anything from buying eco-label products to recycling. If you bought organic food, or ethical investment products or bicycles, or if you separated your waste and took it to recycling centres, you earned points on your plastic Nu-SpaarPas. You could spend them on public transport – as in Curitiba – or theatre tickets, sports training, going to the zoo, education and much else besides.

Like the Commonweal project (see page 181), this funnelled spare capacity into changing people's behaviour. The cost of Nu-SpaarPas was covered by the savings the city made because people delivered their own bulky waste for recycling. Like good neighbourliness, 'green behaviour' takes extra time, but nobody notices, nobody rewards it and nobody thanks you. The Nu-SpaarPas can reward it with the city's spare capacity, being 'efficient' in a way that traditional accountancy with ordinary money doesn't allow.

Nu-SpaarPas ended in 2004, but similar projects are being considered in the UK, waiting until cities have issued their own smartcards for other purposes. There is some evidence that rewarding people for recycling is much more efficient than punishing them for not doing so. London's transport Oyster card could be adapted to encourage sustainability.

Number of outstanding reward points and frequent flyer miles issued in the USA (2007):   14 trillion

Maxine Holdsworth and David Boyle
Carrots Not Sticks
National Consumer Council, 2004

Tradeable energy quotas
Money from the greenhouse effect

"Money should circulate like rainwater."

Thornton Wilder, *The Matchmaker*, 1954

When the greenhouse effect threw up the idea of tradeable carbon emissions permits – now the basis of the international climate change negotiations about how much fossil fuels each nation has the right to burn – it provided a whole new possible basis for money and for international trade.

Imagine, said the policy analyst David Fleming, that those emissions permits are not just credited towards nations, and traded by nations and companies, but credited to all of us as individuals and ordinary businesses, rather like wartime ration coupons. In fact, it was his childhood experiences with sweet rations that gave him the idea that the permits or coupons could be held on a personal smartcard and either spent or traded by individuals, just as they are by nations.

The idea of 'tradeable energy quotas' (TEQs) was introduced for the first time in an article in *Country Life* in 1996, and immediately caught the attention of the European Commission. They were developed further by Richard Starkey at Huddersfield University. But they have an importance beyond simple rationing: by crediting permits to every individual, which they can sell on if they don't need them, the government would be providing a kind of basic citizens' income (see page 104) that favours the most abstemious energy users.

TEQs are intended as a way of involving everyone in reducing our carbon emissions. And in case you don't believe something so elusive could provide the basis for anything that could be bought and sold, it is happening already – and not just in the Chicago exchange that has pioneered carbon trading. Green energy producers on continental Europe are already unbundling the energy from the 'green-ness' – and selling on the green aspect to electricity suppliers in the UK who want to sell green energy to their customers but haven't yet got enough wind turbines and farms to provide it.

The TEQ idea works like this:

• The UK agrees its annual carbon 'budget' through international negotiations; it will reduce over time.
• The 'carbon units' making up the budget are issued to adults, companies and organisations. All adults get the same allocation free, but organisations and companies have to bid for them at an auction held by the government.
• Every time you buy energy – either electricity, gas or petrol – you have to hand over some of your credits on an electronic smartcard.
• If you need more credits, you have to buy them from the national exchange. But if you have been frugal or you have invested in energy-saving improvements at home and reduced your energy consumption, you can sell your credits and make some money – either through ATM machines, over the counter at banks, post offices and energy retailers, or by direct debit arrangements with energy suppliers.

The scheme makes it very clear to people how much fossil fuel can be used in the future. It is also fair. "The instrument gives consumers themselves a central role in the reduction of carbon emissions," says David Fleming. "It does not act over their heads; it involves them. It is therefore transparent: it is clear to consumers how the scheme works, and how prices are set. There is no sense that there is some anonymous government body setting the prices for them. It is the citizens' own scheme; there is a sense of justice."

Number of calories per day allowed for men under rationing in World War II in the UK (creating unprecedented public health): 3,000

www.teqs.net

The future of money
A multi-currency world

"To scatter plenty o'er a smiling land."
Thomas Gray, 'Elegy written in a country churchyard', 1751

The real role of complementary currencies is that they give value to assets which the big international currencies ignore. Maybe they are the effort and time of neighbours (time banks), or almost outdated hotel rooms or surplus stock that would never otherwise be sold (barter exchanges). Maybe they are local skills or local products (local currencies). Wall Street might not regard these as valuable, but they are; these other kinds of money can recognise that value and turn them into the assets they are.

Currencies don't measure very well: what they miss out gets ignored, then forgotten. Then it disappears.

Any kind of money has an information role (medium of exchange) and a value role (store of value) – otherwise it will fail as money. But complementary currencies can change the balance between these two functions. They can be information that can be used to exchange but that may not keep its value, or they can be genuine stores of value which might be less easy or practical to use as small change.

There has been a flurry of new experiments in money. The Dutch internet currency qoin has recently been pioneering online exchanges, following in the path pioneered by beenz and i-points which were victims of the dot.com collapse in 2001.

Some experiments in new currencies designed to keep their value have run into more complicated difficulties. One online currency based on gold, E-gold, fell victim to regulators, and Liberty Dollars – which minted sterling silver versions of the US dollar – was raided by the FBI.

The truth is that different people need different kinds of money, which behave in different ways and value different assets. But we also all need different kinds of money for different aspects of our lives. If we don't get that, some parts of our cities will be rich and some poor, and some parts of our lives will be rich and some poor in the same way.

That is why we need, and will slowly get, a range of currencies – time banks to underpin the social economy, local currencies to keep money and resources circulating locally, regional currencies to provide low-cost finance to small businesses. And we need a range of experimental currencies based on anything from renewable energy to the value of local vegetables.

This is happening already in the currency experiments and barter exchanges springing up around the world. The euro crosses the border from the Republic of Ireland to circulate in Northern Ireland (where the main currency is the pound), just as the US dollar circulates in southern Canada. You can use euros in shops and phone boxes in London. It is only a matter of time before smartcards like Oyster start to hold other kinds of value, and successful websites like eBay and Facebook will start to experiment with currencies too. It will be more complicated, but – just as a multi-currency world worked well in the Middle Ages – so it will make much more possible than a single-currency world.

The green economist Richard Douthwaite proposes four currencies inside one nation:

• An international currency for trading between nations, keeping the global economy within the trading capacity of the planet.
• A national-exchange currency for trading inside a nation, issued interest-free by the central bank, to encourage commercial activity.
• User-controlled currencies, like LETS, time banks and others to underpin different aspects of local life.
• A store-of-value currency, for saving – for houses and other capital assets, linking your savings to the prosperity of the nation.

Average family's energy needs every year: 5,000 kilowatt hours

Richard Douthwaite
The Ecology of Money
Schumacher Briefings, Green Books, 1999

Spiritual money

Is money an expression of spiritual health? Is there another reality behind it that we need to understand? Is there a mysterious way in which the flow of money reflects other kinds of energy? Who knows – but this is another angle on our broadening view of what wealth might mean ...

Does money exist?
You can't take it with you, after all

"Every time a child says 'I don't believe in fairies', there is a little fairy somewhere that falls down dead."

JM Barrie, *Peter Pan*, 1904

The days when you could store all your worldly wealth under the mattress, or under the floorboards like George Eliot's miser Silas Marner, have not entirely disappeared – though it never was a very good idea. Now our world is very different: most of our money exists – in the sense of something we can hold – only in the brief moments when we turn a little of it into cash. The rest of the time it is blips on computers, stored in cyberspace.

If you are wealthy and powerful enough, these blips can be almost infinitely elastic. The Cincinnati investment adviser Paul Herrlinger claimed to be bidding for the Minneapolis store chain Dayton-Hudson for $6.8 billion in 1987 – about $6.7 billion more than the assets of his company. In those heady days, when anyone could borrow anything, he was widely believed on Wall Street and Dayton-Hudson shares climbed $10.

After his lawyer tried to head off disaster by explaining that his client was ill, Herrlinger was asked by TV interviewers on his lawn whether the bid was a hoax. "I don't know," he said. "It's no more a hoax than anything else."

When the sceptical American financial writer James Grant called his book *Money of the Mind* (1994), this is what he meant. We now live in a strange world, after all, where the loan we get from the bank is considered by both lender and borrower as an asset.

But there are other senses in which money doesn't exist. So often our relationship with money is an expression of what is going on inside our minds rather than an objective process. Like everything else in life, if you cling on to it too tightly, it tends to seep away. If you give it away – and most religions urge us to give away or 'tithe' at least ten per cent of our income – it often seems to come back (see page 198).

We also know how much the markets depend on belief to give shares value (see page 122). The value of shares or currencies depends on moods, weather patterns and what traders believe will happen. Belief creates wealth: it keeps the ship afloat – otherwise we could not trust each other enough to exchange money. Belief creates money; cynicism undermines it.

In this sense, debt is a serious spiritual malaise – poised between having and not having – and close to the word 'death' from which it derives. In this sense also, the importance of money is not so much in its substance – most currencies these days are held up by considerable government debt – it is in the energy behind it. Currency comes from the Latin word *currens*, to circulate.

When we believe in it, and when we have relationships with each other, then money circulates and wealth grows. In itself, sitting in the bank, it barely exists at all.

"It takes a village to raise a child. It also takes a village to create money," wrote the Buddhist biologist José Reissig in *New Economics* in 1991. "To be aware of this is to take a crucial step towards making our lives whole. Money cannot exist by itself; it has no value or meaning apart from us. Ultimately, the equation is very simple: we are it."

Amount of gold in the central banks of the world: about enough to fill a semi-detached house.

Deepak Chopra
Creating Affluence: The A to Z Guide to a Richer Life
Bantam Press, 1999

Giving it all away
The thrill of philanthropy

"He who does not give what he has, will not get what he wants."
Henry III, who had this written over the door to the
Painted Chamber in the Palace of Westminster

A million Americans are each set to inherit $1 million or more in
the next 20 years. A terrifying $8,000 billion – the net worth of all
Americans over 50 – will be passing from one generation to the next
within 30 years or so. This may be a bounteous gift from one generation,
but it can also be a frightening burden.

The problem has generated organisations that support people with
inherited wealth – including the Funding Network in London, the
Money Meaning and Choices Institute in San Francisco, and the Boston-
based Impact Project, which actually encourages them to give it away. It
was founded by Anne Slepian and Christopher Mogil, who first realised
he had inherited a great deal of money in 1978, when his stockbroker's
secretary phoned in case he had any questions about his portfolio.

"I was haunted by the question of why I should have this privilege,"
he wrote. "I wondered whether I was selfish, pampering myself and
avoiding my own insecurities about working. At bottom was a fairly
simple question: should I give away my wealth?"

Those who have taken that dramatic step include Millard Fuller, the
founder of Habitat for Humanity, who gave away everything he had
earned to persuade his wife to come back to him. Or Procter & Gamble
heir Robbie Gamble; or Ben Cohen, of Ben & Jerry's ice cream, who tries
to give away as much as he spends. In 1986, he gave away $500,000 of
stock to launch the Ben & Jerry's Foundation.

Other major donors include Bill and Melinda Gates, the legendary
investor Warren Buffett, and the television mogul Ted Turner, who gave
$1 billion to UN projects. Domino Pizza founder Thomas Monaghan
sold his company for a similar amount and gave it away, after reading
CS Lewis's book *Mere Christianity*. Another was James Rouse, the
inventor of the shopping mall.

"I was cared for by a black woman named Gussie from the South Side of Chicago," wrote Edorah Frazer, a teacher who gave away $450,000 – three quarters of her inheritance – in her twenties. "She worked for my family until I was in high school. I always noticed that her clothes were different and that she rode the bus while we drove. My first awareness of class differences came from her presence in our household."

Edorah gave away her wealth in share certificates two days before Christmas. "Outside it was raining, and across the street I saw two Salvation Army men with a bucket ringing a bell. The rain was falling on me and I started to cry. It felt really clean, so simple. Although I was happy, I thought: I'm lonely. I wish I had done this with someone. Then immediately I thought: 'No, it's good that I did it alone, because it is a very individual act.' Ultimately I am alone in this decision. It's my story. I crossed the street, took out all the money in my wallet and put it into the Salvation Army bucket."

Giving it away is a traditional theme in all religions; many encourage their members to give away at least a tenth of what they earn as a tithe. Some say that this kind of giving can release some of the energy about money, and that – if you start doing so – giving can flow back to you. This is of course completely irrational, but so are a lot of things that work.

The traditional Christian view is that belongings should only lie on your shoulders like a light cloak, which can be thrown aside. The cloak became an iron cage, said the pioneer sociologist Max Weber. That is why giving money away can, paradoxically, make you wealthier.

BIGGEST DONORS IN HISTORY:
Warren Buffett: $30 billion
Bill Gates: $29 billion
Li Ka-Shing: $10 billion
George Soros: $6 billion

Christopher Mogil and Anne Slepian
We Gave Away a Fortune
New Society Publishers, 1992

Downshifting
Voluntary simplicity

"Life is frittered away by detail ... simplify, simplify."
Henry David Thoreau, *Walden*, 1854

The management guru Charles Handy tells a story about meeting
an attractive girl at a party, hearing that she is a freelance television
scriptwriter, but then discovering that she has actually only ever sold one
script. "But what do you do for money?" he asks. "Oh, for money I pack
eggs on Sundays."

The point he was making was that people are increasingly defining
themselves not by their jobs, but by their dreams – or something else.
And for many people, dreams do not include working their fingers to
the bone to earn more money than the neighbours. They might be about
deliberately earning less, or just enough to live where they want to.

In many ways, apparently wealthy societies display a hidden misery
and quiet desperation. "People are very empty and they are looking
for much deeper passions in life than those provided through material
accumulation or through vicarious association with status symbols and
people who represent them," said the American futurist Gerald Celente.
The phenomenon of downshifting has emerged as a result.

The mere existence of 'downshifters' is another nail in the coffin of
economic theories which suppose that we all, always, seek to maximise
our income. It is also a testimony to growing resistance to the rat race.
Even at the height of the boom in the richest country in the world – the
USA – there were 7,000 bankruptcies an hour during working hours,
and people were guzzling anti-depressants at an alarming rate.

There have always been people like Tom and Barbara Good from the
BBC sitcom *The Good Life*, but the latest generation of downshifters were
launched by Duane Elgin, the American author of the influential book
Voluntary Simplicity (1981). He defined it as "the deliberate choice to live with
less in the belief that more of life will be returned to us in the process".

Downshifting has become a matter of being less busy, taking more
time, and trying to get off the treadmill to live a bit more authentically,

making relationships more central in our lives. This simple definition of downshifting would mean that up to a quarter of the British and American population were 'downshifters' in one sense or another.

But of all the downshifters, the most fanatical was Amy Dacyczyn. She and her husband Jim had both been working for 20 years – she as a graphic designer, he in the US Navy – but had amassed savings of just $1,500. So in the early 1990s, they set about the task of not spending money, with enormous imagination and enthusiasm. After seven years, they had saved $49,000 from Jim's salary and bought a farmhouse in Maine. But that wasn't the end. Amy put her discoveries into a newsletter called *The Tightwad Gazette*, so that everybody else could benefit from her ideas. By the mid-1990s, she had made such a success of *The Tightwad Gazette* that she was, ironically, rich enough to retire.

Two other organisations that have done more than most to encourage simpler living are the *New Road Map Foundation*, a Seattle-based think tank founded by Joe Dominguez and Vicky Rubin, co-authors of the bestseller *Your Money or Your Life* (1992), which set out how to live a simpler, independent life. The other is Adbusters, the Vancouver-based campaign against consumer advertising and mind control – producing the most extraordinary posters, designed by advertising executives working at night.

These and others have together built one of the most powerful movements in the world, a critique of the way money can undermine 'real wealth', the spiritual rage that underpins the anti-globalisation campaign, and a step-by-step guide to doing something about it in your own life – to have life more abundantly.

Number of Europeans deliberately taking a cut in salary or hours: 12 million
Number opting out of the rat race completely: 2 million

Tracey Smith
The Book of Rubbish Ideas
Sawday's Fragile Earth, 2008

Ethical consumption
Vigilantes in the supermarket aisles

"To live means to buy, to buy means to have power, to have power means to have duties."

National Consumer League motto, 19th century

The idea that people would put their money towards the most ethical buy rather than the cheapest was anathema to free marketeers, yet the success of *The Green Consumer Guide* by John Elkington and Julia Hailes (1988) showed just how much scope there was. When supermarkets realised that up to 40 per cent of their customers would pay more for 'ethical' products – green, organic or fair trade – they hurried to oblige.

The whole phenomenon began with the boycott of South African products under apartheid, and reached a crescendo with the Marine Stewardship Council (conserving fish), the Forest Stewardship Council (sustainable wood) and the Ethical Trading Initiative (tackling sweatshops). The rise of organic food, recycled paper, fairtrade coffee and energy-saving lightbulbs are all testament to the buying power of the ethical consumer.

But ethical consumerism can only go so far by itself. It can punish corporations, as it punished Esso after their efforts to undermine the Kyoto agreement. It can lead to 'fairer' products on the shelves, but people can still only choose the best on offer. It leaves the basic structures, the bogus advertising and the fuel-consuming out-of-town shopping centres, intact. Even so, there have been some successes:

- Lead-free petrol has now driven out anything else.
- Organic food consumption has been growing at the rate of 25 per cent a year in the UK (though it has slowed in the recent credit crunch). Taken together with fairtrade food, the market was up by over a quarter between 2001 and 2002.
- 'Green' mortgages grew by more than 50 per cent in 2002 alone.
- Free-range eggs are increasingly popular, though the market for eggs is dropping generally.

The UK ethical market is now worth about £32 billion a year, having almost doubled in five years. Ethical consumerism can also lead to more sophisticated ideas, such as consumer co-ops and community-supported agriculture (see page 160) and Slow Food.

The Slow Food movement was the brainchild of Carlo Petrini, launched in response to a McDonald's opening in Rome's Piazza di Spagna in 1986. From their headquarters in Bra in Piedmont, at the foot of the Alps – a region known for its truffles and red wine – the Slow Food movement has since taken up the cause of long-tailed sheep of Laticauda, Siennese pigs, Vesuvian apricots and many other half-forgotten foods.

As the market staggers from the credit crunch, it is not yet clear what the effect will be on fairtrade or ethical products, let alone organic and local food, all of which carry a premium. There will inevitably be a dip, but the long-term trend is almost certainly upwards.

Average annual spending per UK household on ethical goods and services (2002): £336
Average annual spending per UK household on ethical goods and services (2007): £664

www.ethicalconsumer.org

Ethical investment
Money as morality

In some ways the best ethical purchase – the one that challenges traditional market assumptions the most – is to invest ethically: not where you get the highest returns, but where you most change the world for the better.

Many trustees and public sector managers certainly believe (though they are not always right) that they have legal duties to get the best returns, regardless of morality. This is often simply conservatism, which used to force anti-smoking organisations to invest in tobacco firms, and peace campaigners to invest in arms manufacturers. Even the Church of England – whose Church Commissioners were endlessly repeating that they were legally obliged to invest for the highest returns – turned out to be investing in the Playboy Channel.

But over the past generation, more people on both sides of the Atlantic have been thinking more carefully about their wealth, making sure it is invested to make the world a better place, or at least no worse. A group of New England Methodists set the ball rolling in 1971 during the Vietnam War by setting up the Pax World mutual fund, which did not invest in weapons. In the UK, ethical investment began formally in 1984 with Friends Provident. Their ethical unit trust was known in the City as the 'Brazil Fund' because it was considered a little 'nutty', but in its first year it was in the top ten performers. There is now nearly £10 billion invested ethically in Britain.

Ethical investment came of age with the launch of the FTSE4Good Index of Ethical Stock, and its American counterpart, the Dow Jones Sustainable Indexes. It has also benefited by new regulations that require investment funds to make a clear statement of their ethical position, if any – which has led a number of funds to be more ethical than they were before.

But one of the peculiarities of the ethical investment world is that it can use a range of different techniques, including:

• **Best of sector investment:** (like FTSE4Good), which means picking the best-behaving company in each sector and investing accordingly. That could mean investing in companies that are really not ethical by any stretch of the imagination, including big oil companies – because it depends entirely on the stage of development in the rest of the sector.
• **Positive ethical investment:** that seeks out genuinely ethical companies to invest in.
• **Ethical engagement:** which means precisely the reverse – choosing companies that are not ethical enough and using the shareholding to put pressure on them.

These different approaches might lead investors to put their money in very different places. What unites them is the ultimate objective: investment returns and leverage on the world. Wherever you put your money, after all, will have an effect on the way the world is and, at the very least, it makes sense to be aware what that effect is.

But ethical investment, and its partner corporate responsibility movement, have both been developing at breakneck speed over the past generation. Both challenge the old idea that business was somehow above ordinary morality and responsibility, and that companies owed duties to shareholders alone. If the economic climate improves, we can expect both to develop further.

There will be more shareholder engagement, aware that – when chief executives earn millions undeservedly – then it is partly a failure of shareholders to exert pressure. There will also be more parallel institutions to raise money for ethical projects, and to sell on those shares. The Ethical Property Company pioneered this as a mainstream idea in the UK, raising £4.2 million in 2002 in a share issue to open more office space for 'social change' organisations.

There will also be more ethical banks: Triodos Bank has branches in four European countries, lending only to ethical projects and businesses. The Aston Reinvestment Trust and the London Rebuilding Society funnel investment money where it is needed the most, and big banks, like the Co-operative Bank, are putting ethics at the heart of everything they do.

We might also expect more local bond issues. Local government is not allowed to issue bonds to raise its own finance in the UK, which is why it so pathetically dependent on central government. But in the USA, local bonds for housing finance are so safe that they are the key element in most people's pensions.

VALUE OF ETHICAL INVESTMENT FUNDS IN THE UK:

1989	£199,000
1995	£792,000
1999	£2.4 million
2002	£4.0 million
2007	£8.9 million

www.ethicalperformance.com
www.triodos.co.uk

Greed therapy
The basis of the problem

"A somewhat disgusting morbidity, one of the semi-criminal, semi-pathological propensities which one hands over with a shudder to the specialists in mental disease."

John Maynard Keynes on the love of money,
Economic Possibilities for our Grandchildren, 1930

It is an old truism that there is enough on the planet for everyone's need but not for everyone's greed. But it is extremely difficult to tell the two apart in practice, because greed is often simply the expression of people's fear that their needs can never be met.

The truth is that money represents considerably more than whatever is written on it. For most of us, it is linked in strange subconscious tangles with love, security, freedom, power and self-worth. This is at least partly because we are never taught – or at least never fully believe – that money is just a means to an end.

The results of greed and its excesses are all around us. American parents in the boom years have been buying their children quarter-sized fully operational Range Rovers ($18,500) for Christmas, or life-sized reproductions of Darth Vader ($5,000), or paying $250,000 for bar-mitzvahs in Manhattan.

But greed may not be quite what it seems. It is barely sane to need more and more and more, and the mega-rich are often those who have an overwhelming fear of poverty that forces them to carry on pushing when any normal human being would sit back and enjoy life. The result is that "money and time are the heaviest burdens of life", according to the 18th-century writer Samuel Johnson, "and the unhappiest of all mortals are those who have more of either than they know how to use".

That is why a new kind of therapy has begun to emerge which helps people tackle their problems with money. Sometimes that relates to their greed – though calling yourself a 'greed therapist' may not encourage customers – but it can also help people confront their money neuroses and the way money divides them from others.

Often this means confronting the most basic beliefs. Even the idea that money means security in old age isn't entirely true: the older people who are most secure are not necessarily those who are financially independent; they are those who can rely on being part of a supportive family and neighbourhood (see page 186).

In most couples for example, one will play the role of the hoarder and one the role of the spender – sometimes playing different roles in different relationships. Often they actually secretly admire the other's ability to hoard or to spend, but daren't admit it, in case it encourages them to go wild or become more miserly.

The key point is that money can never represent actual love or security; it is just money, after all. But if people fail to engage greed therapists, then one idea from the economist Robert Frank might have an effect: a 70 per cent 'Additional Consumption Tax' on outrageous luxuries like the mini Range Rover.

Average time spent shopping per week in the USA: 6 hours
Average time spent playing with children per week in the USA: 40 minutes

Dorothy Rowe
The Real Meaning of Money
HarperCollins, 1997

Alchemy
The lure of the philosopher's stone

"The only thing money cannot buy is meaning."
Jacob Needleman, *Money and the Meaning of Life*, 1991

The 13th-century pioneer of chemistry, Roger Bacon, explained that alchemy "teaches us how to make the noble metals and colours and many other things better and more copiously by art than they can be made by nature". It is more important than other sciences, he went on, "since it produces most useful products, giving not only the monies and other expenses of the state, but the wherewithal to prolong life".

At its best, alchemy was about effecting change – about changing and perfecting people as much as changing metals. It was about using what we have to create wealth, in its broadest sense. As the Middle Ages went by, alchemy also gained a radical edge. Alchemists like the mysterious Paracelsus – wandering round Europe in a coloured coat which he never washed – were the inspiration behind a Protestant revolution against the old order of authority and control.

They threatened the old certainties of medicine and politics with their dreams of a 'chemical revolution' which would restore humanity, attacking monopolies and putting power and medical knowledge in the hands of ordinary people. And now, five centuries on, there is a new kind of alchemy emerging, working out how to take everyday assets – skills, care, abilities, forgotten resources that the narrow economy fails to recognise – and using them to enhance life. This is a demonstration, at every level of society, that by working together we can all create the equivalent of gold.

It is another Protestant revolution of a kind, which says that the solution to the problem is not to hand over more power to the priests (the bankers) to create money for us, still less to the king (the government) to do it – but to find ways that we can create the money we need ourselves. It also recognises that for the word 'wealth' to mean anything at all, we are going to have to go a long way beyond mere money.

PARACELSUS ON ALCHEMY (*FROM ALCHEMICAL CATECHISM*, c1520)

Question: When the philosophers speak of gold and silver, from which they extract their matter, are we to suppose that they refer to the vulgar gold and silver?

Answer: By no means; vulgar silver and gold are dead, while those of the philosophers are full of life.

Conclusion

"Once we allow ourselves to be disobedient to the test of an accountant's profit, we have begun to change our civilisation."

John Maynard Keynes, *National Self-sufficiency*, 1933

"Our deepest fear is not that we are powerless. Our deepest fear is that we are powerful beyond measure."

Nelson Mandela, 1994, quoting from 'Our Greatest Fear' by
Marianne Williamson, *Return to Love*, 1992

As I come to the end of this book, the money system has become more visibly insane. Shell-shocked investors are photographed with their heads in their hands, or carrying their belongings home in a cardboard box. Traders are seen screaming in panic as the markets plummet. The US Treasury Secretary goes down on his knees to the Speaker of the House of Representatives in Washington, begging her to pass what amounts to the biggest state intervention in history.

Something will change, but there is no point in being naïve. Markets have crashed before but the same old system has reappeared in a slightly different form. We may be at the beginning of a new era when money is re-forged to meet all our needs, to bend the system so that it enhances life. Instead, it will probably continue its dedication to the task of making a handful of people terrifyingly rich.

I am not exactly pessimistic. The system will continue because of faults that lie much deeper in money than anything that a flurry of regulation can change. That has been the message of this book, weaving through the various stories. It amounts to this:

1. There is a fundamental moral problem about the way we use money: it isn't immoral, but it is amoral – it over-values unimportant things (fast food franchises, foreign exchange, hedge funds), and under-values important things (families, communities, nurses).
2. Because of this, money acts with ferocious power to fling aside privilege based on land or aristocracy. In that sense, it is the creator of the modern 'liberal' world. But it doesn't stop there: it carries on

corroding, driving out community, family and spirituality, if we let it.
It tends to drive out what is best, urgent and vital. It downvalues variety,
diversity and creativity, leaving just money behind, paving a valueless
paradise to put up a parking lot that fits on a set of accounts.

3. It is hopelessly unfair in its rules. It is flexible, subsidised, endlessly
available and forgiving to the wealthy, while it is concrete, scarce and
unforgiving to everyone else. It creates its own aristocracy and looks
after them. Because of that, it is both over-abundant for the useless
and luxurious, yet running dangerously scarce for the vital things in
life – because useless but lucrative investments where money breeds on
money suck it all up, and we find that the money for real things gets
whittled away.

In other words, the conclusion is the same as John Ruskin's in 1860:
there is no wealth but life. But the danger is becoming clearer every
year. People who want to produce books or grow barley or sell food now
have to do so through the gaps, and with the crumbs that are the by-
products of speculation, because the financial carousel that spins above
us all produces nothing real. One day, it may be impossible to produce
anything else.

It is a very practical problem, especially as the world constantly
teeters on the edge of financial crisis, and we may eventually find that
the combination of electronic capital, just-in-time delivery systems and
high-energy technocracy is unable to deliver what we need. Even when
the financial world is working perfectly, in its own terms, most of us still
find ourselves on the outside, using imagination and initiative to live
fulfilled and human lives.

Once again, the problem is also primarily a moral one, which no
amount of legislation can solve. People in every age have confused
money with real value, and they probably always will, but it would
certainly be pessimistic to end the story there.

The hope lies in our own collusion with money and our joint
responsibility for the problem. The 'original sin' of interest may be
laying waste to the planet because it demands such high growth and
high returns, but most of us are implicated in it with our savings, our
mortgages and our pensions. The monster corporations may dominate
so much of our lives, and may – despite their 'social responsibility' –

be corroding planet, food and culture as their core business. But we collude by giving them our money, sometimes because we now have no alternative, but often because it is simply easier.

Money is not as good a measuring system as it claims to be. When it comes to the fundamentals of life, it is practically blind. But we are not blind. As human beings, we can see more clearly, and take responsibility at least for our part.

We can persuade the government to issue more money interest-free, rather than letting banks create it all. We can make sure, either through laws or taxes, that the full costs of enterprises are reflected in prices, that subsidies for unsustainable activities end and that polluters pay for their damage. We can find ways to make money circulate better in local communities without seeping out to distant corporations. We can try to make sure that nobody gets paid – for the sake of argument – more than a hundred times more than anyone else. It doesn't sound much, does it?

But we can also beware of expecting governments to act when we do nothing ourselves. That means staying a little sceptical of catch-all solutions that are supposed to solve everything, whether they are land tax or monetary reform. There may be a place for a measure of both, but they will never change the world by themselves, because the fundamental problem is this ancient mismatch between money and value. The law of unintended consequences hangs heavy over single solutions, and we should beware of them, if only because they expect governments to solve the problems and appear to absolve us of our continuing responsibility.

Centralisation and monopoly have always tended towards tyranny and monoculture, and that is the problem with money too.

That means playing our own part in opting out of the monoculture economy when we can. Big currencies, and big global systems, tend towards monoculture; they drive out anything different, whether they are other languages, other cultures or other species. An economy that is human and real is one with a diversity of measuring systems, and that means a diversity of kinds of money, not neatly segregated by national boundaries, but overlapping.

That means using as diverse a range of currencies as we can, as locally as we can, and remembering that no money, however diverse, will ever encompass the most important things in life, because they are not susceptible to measurement. Love, health, joy, beauty will never be monetised, though diverse money systems might help us to spread them more widely.

But most important of all, there are things we can do as individuals to tackle the money system at its most corrupt, and they are all to do with making wealth, money, places and life real and human again:

Real, human wealth

We may not be able to turn money values on their heads, at least by ourselves. But we can buy and invest according to what is most human. We can buy what is made locally, made by craftspeople and small producers, or invest in projects that will help such people, not where the financial experts, the marketeers or the markets urge us to invest. We can buy fairtrade goods direct from the people that make them. We can use our intuition, and inform ourselves about which global brands are owned by which global monsters, and withdraw our support from companies that lay waste the Earth and its inhabitants. We have a vote in the global marketplace – our buying power – and we should use it.

Real, human places

We have choice about what kind of places our high streets and towns become, and we can use our time and money accordingly. We can shun fast food and mega-malls, and take our custom whenever we can to shops and restaurants that are owned locally. And when we cannot avoid fast food and modern machine systems, we can at least chat to the poor de-humanised staff behind the counters. When we use supermarkets, we can demand that they have a choice of fruit and vegetables from the country in which they are operating. We can weave back together the intricate local systems of mutual support.

Real, human money

We may not be able to stop the dematerialisation of money, but then that isn't really the point. We can help the spread of diverse new kinds of money to underpin a diverse world. We can innovate with the points systems of big corporations, use them in ways that weren't intended – trading Nectar points or donating them to charity. We can use local currencies and, where they are not available, we can barter or give things away. We can join our local time bank, and join any local system that supports and funds local food or local production.

Real, human life
Again, we can't stand up by ourselves against the weight of the system, but we can – just by working on our own lives – hold out against it, and maybe by example motivate others to do so. We can encourage simplicity and creativity. We can put our relationships and our creative lives a little higher in our list of priorities. We can give more, and sometimes maybe even accept more in return. We can do things for free, we can surprise people by our semi-independence from the financial world. We can find and celebrate the inner wealth in people that the market sidelines – and in ourselves.

These are all hard to do, for me as much as for everybody else. We can never transform the financial system by ourselves, but we can make a difference and encourage other people to claw back humanity from flawed money, and feel a little 'wealthier' as a result.

David Boyle
Crystal Palace
April 2009

Bibliography

Introduction
Ruskin, John, *Unto This Last*, 1860
(Penguin Classics 2005)

Section I
Metal money

Bloom, William, *Money, Heart and Mind*,
Penguin, 1996

Borsodi, Ralph, *Inflation and the Coming
Keynesian Catastrophe*, EF Schumacher
Society, 1989

Davies, Glyn, *A History of Money*,
University of Wales Press, 1994

Ekins, Paul; Hillman, Mayer, and
Hutchison, Robert, *Wealth Beyond
Measure: An atlas of new economics*,
Gaia Books, 1992

Galbraith, John K, *Money: Whence it
came, where it went*, Penguin, 1975

Grant, James, *Money of the Mind*, Farrar,
Strauss and Giroux, 1994

Hancock, Graham, *The Lords of Poverty*,
Macmillan, 1989

Jacobs, Jane, *Cities and the Wealth of
Nations: Principles of economic life*,
Penguin, 1986

Keynes, John Maynard, 'National Self-
Sufficiency', *The Yale Review* vol 22, 4:
June 1933

Klein, Naomi, *The Shock Doctrine: The rise
of disaster capitalism*, Allen Lane, 2007

Korten, David C, *When Corporations Rule
the World*, Kumarian Press, 1995

Krugman, Paul, 'Who Was Milton
Friedman?', *New York Review of Books*
vol 54, 2: 15 February 2007

Mill, John Stuart, *On Liberty*, 1859
(Oxford Paperbacks 2008)

Mill, John Stuart, *Principles of Political
Economy*, 1848
(Prometheus Books 2004)

Palmer, Henry and Conaty, Pat,
Profiting from Poverty, New Economics
Foundation, 2003

Reeves, Richard, *John Stuart Mill:
Victorian firebrand*, Atlantic Books, 2007

Rueff, Jacques, *The Age of Inflation*, trans.
AH Meeus and FG Clarke, Henry Regnery
Co, 1964

Schopenhauer, Arthur, *Counsels and
Maxims*, 1788–1860
(Hard Press 2006)

Smith, Adam, *The Wealth of Nations*,
1776 (Bantam Classics 2003)

Strathern, Paul, *A Brief History of
Economic Genius*, Texere, 2002

Wolfe, Tom, *The Bonfire of the Vanities*,
Bantam Books, 1987

Section II
Information money

Barlow, John Perry, 'The Economy of Ideas', *Wired* issue 2.03: March 1994

Bernstein, Peter L, *Against the Gods: The remarkable story of risk*, John Wiley & Sons, 1997

Boyle, David, *Why London needs its own currency*, New Economics Foundation, 2000

Buchan, James, *Frozen Desire*, Picador, 1997

Gray, John, *False Dawn: The delusions of global capitalism*, Granta Books, 1998

Keynes, John Maynard, *The Economic Consequences of the Peace*, 1919 (BiblioBazaar 2007)

Keynes, John Maynard, *General Theory of Employment, Interest and Money*, Macmillan, 1936

Kurtzman, Joel, *The Death of Money*, Simon & Schuster, 1993

Lietaer, Bernard, *The Future of Money*, Century, 2001

Partnoy, Frank, *F.I.A.S.C.O*, WW Norton & Company, 1997

Roddick, Anita, *Take it Personally: How globalization affects you and how to fight back*, Thorsons, 2001

Rowe, Dorothy, *The Real Meaning of Money*, HarperCollins Publishers, 1997

Singh, Kavaljit, *Taming Global Capital Flows: Challenges and Alternatives in the Era of Financial Globalisation*, Zed Books, 2000

Woods, Brett F (editor), *Letters From France: The private diplomatic correspondence of Benjamin Franklin 1776–1785*, Algora Publishing, 2007

Section III
Measuring money

Adams, John, *Cost–Benefit Analysis: Part of the problem, not the solution*, Green College Centre for Environmental Policy and Understanding, 1995

Boyle, David, *The Tyranny of Numbers*, HarperCollins/Flamingo, 2001

Crosby, Alfred, *The Measure of Reality: Quantification and Western society 1250–1600*, Cambridge University Press, 1997

Ekins, Paul; Hillman, Mayer, and Hutchison, Robert, *Wealth Beyond Measure: An atlas of new economics*, Gaia Books, 1992

Elkington, John, and Hailes, Julia, *The Green Consumer Guide*, Victor Gollancz, 1988

Ford, Henry, *Today and Tomorrow*, 1926 (Productivity Press 1988)

Galbraith, John K, *The Great Crash* 1929, 1955 (Houghton Mifflin, 1997)

Jacobs, Jane, *The Death and Life of Great American Cities*, Random House, 1961

Keynes, John Maynard, 'National Self-Sufficiency', *The Yale Review* vol 22, 4: June 1933

Kuznets, Simon, 'How to Judge Quality', *The New Republic*, 20 October 1962

MacGillivray, Alex; Weston, Candy, and Unsworth, Catherine, *Communities Count! A step-by-step guide to community sustainability indicators*, New Economics Foundation, 1998

Marks, Nic, et al., *The Happy Planet Index*, New Economics Foundation, 2006

Myers, Norman and Kent, Jennifer, *Perverse Subsidies: How misused tax dollars harm the environment and the economy*, Island Press, 2001

Pearce, David and Barbier, Edward B, *Blueprint for a Sustainable Economy*, Earthscan, 2000

Porritt, Jonathon, *Capitalism as if the World Matters*, Earthscan, 2005

Shaw, George Bernard, *John Bull's Other Island,* 1904 (1st World Library, 2004)

Simms, Andrew, *Five Brothers: The Rise and Nemesis of the Big Bean Counters*, New Economics Foundation, 2002

Waring, Marilyn, *If Women Counted: A new feminist economics*, HarperCollins, 1989

Section IV
Debt money

A Green New Deal: Joined-up policies to solve the triple crunch of the credit crisis, climate change and high oil prices, New Economics Foundation, 2008

Boyle, David (editor), *The Money Changers: Currency reform from Aristotle to e-cash*, Earthscan, 2002

Douglas, Clifford Hugh, *Economic Democracy*, 1920 (Kessinger Publishing, 2008)

Ekins, Paul, Hillman, Mayer, and Hutchison, Robert, *Wealth Beyond Measure: An atlas of new economics*, Gaia Books, 1992

Flurscheim, Michael, *Clue to the Economic Labyrinth*, Swan Sonnenschein, 1902

Hutchinson, Frances, *What Everybody Really Wants to Know about Money*, Jon Carpenter, 1998

Kennedy, Margrit and Kennedy, Declan, *Interest and Inflation Free Money*, New Society Publishers, 1995

Keynes, John Maynard, *General Theory of Employment, Interest and Money*, Macmillan, 1936

Lietaer, Bernard, *The Future of Money*: *A new way to create wealth, work and a wiser world*, Century, 2001

Newton, Lisa H, *Permission to Steal: Revealing the roots of corporate scandal*, Blackwell Publishing, 2006

Pettifor, Ann, *The Coming First World Debt Crisis*, Palgrave Macmillan, 2006

Robertson, James, and Huber, Joseph, *Creating New Money: A monetary reform for the information age*, New Economics Foundation, 2000

Rowbotham, Michael, *The Grip of Death: A study of modern money, debt slavery and destructive economics*, Jon Carpenter, 1998

Yunus, Muhammad, *Banker to the Poor: The autobiography of Muhammad Yunus, founder of the Grameen Bank*, Aurum Press, 1998

Section V
Mad money

Burrough, Bryan and Helyar, John, *Barbarians at the Gate: The fall of RJR Nabisco*, Harper & Row, 1990

Cassidy, John, *Dot.con: The greatest story ever sold*, HarperCollins, 2002

Chancellor, Edward, *Devil Take the Hindmost: A history of financial speculation*, Farrar, Straus and Giroux, 1999

Elliott, Larry and Atkinson, Dan, *The Gods That Failed: How Blind Faith in Markets Has Cost Us Our Future*, Bodley Head, 2008

Galbraith, John K, *The Great Crash 1929*, 1955 (Houghton Mifflin, 1997)

Gates, Jeff, *Democracy at Risk: Rescuing Main Street from Wall Street*, Perseus, 2000

Grant, James, *Grant's Interest Rate Observer*, 2008

Grant, James, *The Trouble with Prosperity*, Crown Business, 1996

Karl, Terry Lynn, *The Paradox of Plenty: Oil booms and petro-states*, University of California Press, 1997

Keynes, John Maynard, 'The Great Slump of 1930', *The Nation and Athenaeum*, 20 and 27 December 1930

MacKay, Charles, *Extraordinary Popular Delusions and the Madness of Crowds*, 1841 (Harriman House 2003)

Morris, Charles, *The Trillion Dollar Meltdown: Easy money, high rollers, and the great credit crash*, Public Affairs, 2008

Reuter, Peter and Truman, Edwin, *Chasing Dirty Money: The fight against money laundering*, Institute for International Economics, 2004

Shiva, Vandana, *Stolen Harvest: The hijacking of the global food supply*, South End Press, 2000

Soros, George, *Soros on Soros*, John Wiley & Sons, 1995

Temple, Peter, *Hedge Funds: The courtesans of capital*, John Wiley & Sons, 2001

Section VI
Local money

Power Hungry: Six reasons to regulate global food corporations, ActionAid, 2005

Belloc, Hilaire, *The Servile State, 1912* (Cosimo Classics 2007)

Chesterton, GK, *The Outline of Sanity*, Methuen, 1926
Galbraith, John K, *The Great Crash 1929*, 1955 (Houghton Mifflin, 1997)

Hopkins, Rob, *The Transition Town Handbook: From oil dependency to local resilience*, Green Books, 2008

Klein, Naomi, *No Logo*, Knopf Canada, 2000

Sacks, Justin, *The Money Trail: Measuring your impact on the local economy using LM3*, New Economics Foundation, 2002

Shiva, Vandana, *Earth Democracy: Justice, sustainability and peace*, South End Press, 2005

Stein, Gertrude, *Everybody's Autobiography,* 1937 (Exact Change 2004)

Section VII
DIY money

Borsodi, Ralph, *Inflation is Coming*, B Lane, 1945

Boyle, David, *Funny Money: In search of alternative cash*, HarperCollins, 1999

Cahn, Edgar, *No More Throw-away People: The co-production imperative*, Essential Books, 2000

de Bono, Edward, *The IBM Dollar*, Centre for the Study of Financial Innovation, 1994

Douthwaite, Richard, *The Ecology of Money*, Green Books, 1999

Douthwaite, Richard, *Short Circuit: Strengthening local economies for security in an unstable world*, Lilliput Press, 1996

Fleming, David, 'Stopping the Traffic', *Country Life* vol 140, 19: 9 May 1996

Greco, Thomas, *Money: Understanding and creating alternatives to legal tender*, Chelsea Green, 2001

Holdsworth, Maxine and Boyle, David, *Carrots Not Sticks*, National Consumer Council, 2004

Jacobs, Jane, *Cities and the Wealth of Nations: Principles of economic life*, Random House, 1984

Neal, Terry L and Eisler, Gary K, *Barter and the Future of Money*, Master Media, 1996

North, Peter, *Money and Liberation: the micropolitics of alternative currency movements*, University of Minnesota Press, 2007

Smith, Adam, *The Wealth of Nations*, 1776 (Bantam Classics 2003)

Watts, Alan, *From time to eternity*, 1960

Section VIII
Spiritual money

Chopra, Deepak, *Creating Affluence: The A to Z Guide to a Richer Life*, Bantam Press 1999

Dominguez, Joe and Rubin, Vicky, *Your Money or Your Life*, 1992 (Penguin updated edition 2008)

Elgin, Duane, *Voluntary Simplicity*, 1981 (HarperCollins revised edition 1993)

Elkington, John and Hailes, Julia, *The Green Consumer Guide*, Victor Gollancz, 1988

Grant, James, *Money of the Mind*, Farrar, Straus and Giroux, 1994

Keynes, John Maynard, 'Economic Possibilities for our Grandchildren', *The Nation and Athenaeum*: 11 and 18 October 1930 (Entropy Conservationists 1987)

Lewis, CS, *Mere Christianity*, Macmillan, 1952

Mogil, Christopher and Slepian, Anne, *We Gave Away a Fortune*, New Society Publishers, 1992

Needleman, Jacob, *Money and the Meaning of Life*, Currency/Doubleday, 1991

Paracelsus, *Alchemical Catechism,* c 1520 (Holmes Publishing Group 1983)

Reissig, José, 'Bonds That Brought a Boom', *New Economics* no 20: Winter 1991

Rowe, Dorothy, *The Real Meaning of Money*, HarperCollins Publishers, 1997

Smith, Tracey, *The Book of Rubbish Ideas*, Sawday's Fragile Earth, 2008

Thoreau, Henry David, *Walden*, 1854 (Oxford Paperbacks 2008)

Conclusion
Keynes, John Maynard, 'National Self-Sufficiency', *The Yale Review* vol 22, 4: June 1933

Internet resources

All web addresses correct when accessed 20 January 2009

Section I   Metal money

Bank of England	www.bankofengland.co.uk
Federal Reserve	www.federalreserve.gov
IMF reform	www.halifaxinitiative.org
Roy Davies, money history	www.project.exeter.ac.uk/RDavies/arian/money.html
World Bank reform	www.brettonwoodsproject.org

Section II   Information money

Alaska Permanent Fund	www.apfc.org
Bernard Lietaer	www.transaction.net/money/bio/lietaer.html
Consult Hyperion (e-cash)	www.hyperion.co.uk
Financial scandals	www.project.exeter.ac.uk/RDavies/arian/scandals
Global Policy Forum	www.globalpolicy.org
GRAIN (biodiversity)	www.grain.org
Institute for Policy Study	www.ips-dc.org
Internat. Forum Globalisation	www.ifg.org
Multinational Monitor	www.essential.org
World Trade Organisation	www.wto.org
Yes! (positive futures)	www.yesmagazine.org

Section III   Measuring money

Andrew Oswald (happiness)	www.oswald.co.uk
Bowling Alone (social capital)	www.bowlingalone.com
Environmental indicators	www.sustainablemeasures.com
ISEA (social auditing)	www.accountability21.net
New Economics Foundation	www.neweconomics.org
Redefining Progress	www.rprogress.org
Securities & Exchange Cssn	www.sec.gov

Section IV   Debt money

Citizen's Income	www.citizensincome.org
Grameen Bank	www.grameen-info.org
Institute for Fiscal Studies	www.ifs.org.uk
Jubilee Debt Campaign	www.jubileedebtcampaign.org.uk
Micro-credit virtual library	www.gdrc.org/icm/
Odious debts	www.odiousdebts.org
Pensions Ombudsman	www.pensions-ombudsman.org.uk
Prosperity UK	www.prosperityuk.com
Social Credit Secretariat	www.douglassocialcredit.com

Section V   Mad money

Charles MacKay (delusions)	www.econlib.org/library/Mackay/macEx.html
Corporate Predators	www.corporatepredators.org